Magickal

Astrology

Magickal

Astrology

Understanding Your Place in the Cosmos

By

Skye Alexander

NEW PAGE BOOKS
A division of The Career Press, Inc.
Franklin Lakes, NJ

MAGICKAL ASTROLOGY
Cover design by Diane Y. Chin
Cover image courtesy: PhotoDisc
Typesetting by Eileen Munson
Printed in the U.S.A. by Book-mart Press

To order this title, please call toll-free 1-800-CAREER-1 (NJ and Canada: 201-848-0310) to order using VISA or Master- Card, or for further information on books from Career Press.

The Career Press, Inc., 3 Tice Road, PO Box 687, Franklin Lakes, NJ 07417
www.careerpress.com
www.newpagebooks.com

Library of Congress Cataloging-in-Publication Data

Alexander, Skye.
    Magickal astrology : understanding your place in the cosmos / by Skye Alexander.
        p. cm.
    Includes bibliographical references and index.
    ISBN 1-56414-479-8 (pbk.)
    1. Magic. 2. Astrology. I. Title.

BF161 .A44 2000
133.4'3—dc21   00-032884

In memory of my second father,

Ray Dell Britton

1923 - 1999

Acknowledgments

I am indebted to Sirona Knight, without whom this book would not exist, and to my editor Mike Lewis. Many thanks to all my friends and colleagues who assisted and encouraged me, especially Kitty Spitzer, and of course, Domino.

Contents

Introduction

"The quest for meaning always takes us into the unknown."
—F. Aster Barnwell

No one knows when human beings began using astrology and magick. Egyptian star charts dating back to 4200 B.C.E. have been found, although some studies suggest that our ancestors tracked lunar cycles as early as 32,000 years ago. Magickal practices are described in ancient texts such as the *I Ching* and the *Upanishads* and abound in the ageless myths of every culture. Cave paintings may have actually been a form of magick, created to petition spirit animals for assistance in hunting. My guess is that this wisdom has always been with us and we are only beginning to remove the shroud of fear and superstition that has hidden it for millennia.

The Interweaving of Astrology and Magick

Astrology and magick are links between universal forces and earthly experience. Like myth, meditation, and art, they provide windows through which we can glimpse the Divine and see its hand shaping the manifest world.

St. Thomas Aquinas believed that "the celestial bodies are the cause of all that takes place in the sublunar world." Astrological forces exert a profound influence on the everyday impulses and activities of human beings, as well as the functioning of the natural world. Not surprisingly, magick, which utilizes the energies of the heavens, nature, and the human psyche, has woven astrology into its fabric. We see this interconnectedness reflected in the symbols, practices, and teachings of various magickal traditions—the sephiroth of the Kabbalistic Tree of Life, the Hindu chakras, the angelic hosts, the tarot, geomancy's signs, and the Rose Cross of the Golden Dawn, to name just a few.

Astrology and magick neither endorse nor reject any spiritual path, although some schools of thought are rooted in specific cultural and/or religious traditions. Most astrologers and magicians support the belief that all quests for truth lead to the same end. In the past, due largely to fear of persecution, access to secret societies and teachings was restricted. Today occult information is widely available in bookstores and online, enabling any seeker to study astrology and magick and to pursue his/her own path, alone or with a group of like-minded individuals.

Many schools of thought exist in both astrology and magick. Astrologers and magicians don't necessarily limit themselves to one school; they may use different systems in different circumstances or combine elements from more than one tradition in their work. None is "right" or "wrong"—all are valid. They all "work." As you learn more and put your knowledge into practice, you'll naturally gravitate toward the path that is most appropriate for you. However, the first path you take may not be the same one you continue on. I urge you to experiment. Bill Whitcomb's encyclopedic guide, *The Magician's Companion*, outlines the basics of numerous mystery traditions and offers extensive bibliographic information for further study into areas that intrigue you.

The astrological information contained in this book is of the contemporary Western tropical variety. This does not mean I discount Chinese or Vedic or heliocentric astrology, only that I am a contemporary Western practitioner who, after more than two decades of study, finds this system to be the most effective for my purposes. Most of the magickal information I've included is akin to neo-Pagan and Wiccan traditions, because these are harmonious with my Celtic heritage, my feminist leanings, my Aquarian dislike of rigid hierarchy, and my love of nature. But I also use feng shui extensively, along with some Eastern yogic practices, the *I Ching*, some American Indian wisdom teachings and shamanic journeying, and some Golden Dawn-style rituals. I share with you what works for me and encourage you to use what you like, reject what you don't, and alter it, expand upon it, and put your own individual stamp on it.

To Believe or Not to Believe

One of the first questions people ask when they learn that I'm an astrologer is, "Do you really believe in that stuff?" No, I explain. Belief requires blind faith in something you can't justify with actual data and predictable results, such as belief in a Divine Power. Astrology's accuracy and usefulness have been demonstrated in countless ways for centuries. I've witnessed its validity time and again in my own life and in the lives of hundreds of other people.

Of course, most people's knowledge of astrology does not extend beyond the horoscopes they read in their daily newspapers. The fact that these superficial columns usually appear on the comics page should tell you something—they are just for fun, the astrological equivalent of fortune cookies. "Real" astrology is a complex art and science, and proficiency in it requires many years of study as well as a certain innate aptitude. Marc Edmund Jones, one of the great practitioners of the modern era, said he'd studied astrology for 50 years and barely scratched the surface.

If human beings weren't such unique and intricate creatures, astrology might be even more "accurate." Free will—the ability to make choices based on our individual levels of awareness—affects how we respond to and utilize cosmic energies, making it tricky for astrologers to predict events with absolute certainty. Still, people generally respond in calculable ways to planetary influences, and the more we understand about these influences, the more control we have over our lives. As astrologers are fond of saying, the stars don't compel, they impel.

Conversely, when I tell people I practice magick, they rarely express skepticism. Everyone, it seems, believes in magick. And most are afraid of it. (My former husband worried that my magickal work led me to associate with unsavory people, that I was inviting trouble, and that I might put unpleasant spells on him.) We've been taught to think of magick as something evil and dangerous, and of magicians as malicious creatures who hex anyone they don't like. *Webster's Ninth New Collegiate Dictionary* erroneously defines "witch" as "one that is credited with malignant supernatural powers; esp. a woman practicing black witchcraft often with the aid of a devil or familiar."

It is true that magick can be dangerous if misused. So can cars and electricity. Magick can also work in mysterious ways. The universe acts according to its own rules and schedule, not ours, and its agenda may include conditions that you couldn't foresee or plan for. A very real caveat of magick is that you must be careful what you wish for—you are likely to get it. Even if you ask for something you really want and do it in the proper manner, harming no one, using qualifying statements and cautions, the results may not be what you expected. I have a healthy respect for magick, just as I do for the ocean, and recommend that you not stray beyond a depth that is comfortable for you in either case.

"Reality" Check

I'm inclined to agree with Vladimir Nabokov, who wrote that "the word, 'reality,' must always be used with quotations." While absolute truth may exist, it is unknowable to human beings. Like blind men describing an elephant, our truths are filtered through our limited perspectives, social conditioning, and individual experiences.

Our ideas influence events; there is no such thing as objective reality. According to Bill Whitcomb, "You cannot observe a phenomenon without altering it by your mode of perception. There is no such thing as an independent observer. You participate in creating the world by perceiving it." This is the basis for working magick.

Refusing to believe the possibility of something's existence can inhibit your ability to see or experience it—but it will not negate its existence or validity. This is particularly true when working in the unseen worlds and with subtle energies, where the rules aren't the same as those of ordinary, material existence.

An open mind is the only prerequisite to studying astrology and magick. If you deny the basic tenets of astrology and magick—that all things are connected, that there are many levels of existence and intelligence beyond what we perceive with our physical senses, that our thoughts can and do affect situations—you're unlikely to make much progress and may end up "proving" to yourself that these things are indeed hokum. Of course, if you weren't already open to such ideas, you probably wouldn't be reading this book!

Chapter 1

As Above, So Below

"Astrology is astronomy brought to Earth and applied to the affairs of men."

—Ralph Waldo Emerson

Most of us living in the 21st century have become detached from the natural and cosmic forces that surround us and permeate our very existence. However, we need only look beneath the surface to see astrology's influence mirrored in virtually every facet of life here on earth, such as architecture, language, medicine, music, art, and mathematics.

This is because our ancestors envisioned heaven and earth as entwined, like the warp and woof threads in a piece of cloth, rather than as separate layers of existence the way we do today. In their conception of the universe, the actions of the celestial bodies influenced everything that happened on this planet. Not only were they aware that the moon's phases affected the tides and that the earth's changing relationship to the sun brought about the seasons, they believed "spirit," or divine energy, penetrated everything on earth and that physical existence was animated by metaphysical forces.

Early cultures perceived the heavenly bodies and the forces of nature as deities. The ancient Egyptians, for instance, interpreted the sky as the goddess Nut, who arched her star-spangled body over the earth, depicted as the god Geb. From their union all of creation evolved. The Japanese Shinto knew the sun as the goddess Amaterasu, whose retreat into the cave of the heavens caused night to descend on earth. Foremost in the Roman pantheon were the gods and goddesses whose names we still associate with the planets. To honor these divine entities, our ancestors built temples, celebrated festivals, created art, composed myths, and paid homage in their daily practices.

Modern materialists tend to discount this view as primitive superstition. But the truth is early cultures—probably because they lived in close contact with the natural world and their survival depended to a large extent on attuning themselves to these forces—understood the magickal workings of the earth and the cosmos more intimately, and in some ways more accurately, than we do today. This knowledge allowed our forebears to move in harmony with the rhythms of the universe instead of struggling against them.

Awe-inspiring structures such as Stonehenge and the pyramids, which still baffle modern scientists, suggest that early cultures were able to utilize forces beyond our current understanding. Did ancient magicians know how to manipulate etheric energies or commune with elemental spirits in the rocks? Did these long-ago builders receive help from divine sources? If we can rediscover the hidden wisdom that has been lost over the centuries and reconnect with the magickal forces around us, who knows what wonders we might achieve today.

Astrology and Architecture

Before churches, mosques, and temples as we know them today existed, nature-oriented cultures designated special places on earth as sacred sites. These spots were chosen because of their affinities with certain gods, goddesses, and planetary deities. Later civilizations erected religious structures at these ancient places of power, such as England's Glastonbury Abbey, which was built on the Pagan sacred site known as Avalon.

Architect and astrologer A.T. Mann explains that, "The sun, moon, planets, and stars were gods and goddesses.... Each deity was associated with a particular planetary body, and its activities and worship were related to the cycle of that body, the apparent movement of the body, and any proportions used to describe its movements or position. To evoke the god, one had to create manifestations of the cycle or numbers associated with the related luminary, planet or star." Temples to the Egyptian god Osiris, for instance, held 365 offering tables, one for each day of the year.

According to Mann, "Most early monuments and temples were aligned to the luminary, planet or star corresponding to the deity to be worshipped." Often a building was oriented so that the rising sun shone into the entrance on the holy day associated with the temple's special deity. The Temple Luxor in Egypt is an interesting example and shows a sophisticated understanding of astronomical movements. Because it was constructed over a period of centuries, the angle of the hall of pillars shifts to align with the changing position of the sun's light as precession of the equinoxes altered the earth's relationship to the heavens.

Stonehenge is one of the best examples of astrology's important role in the ancient world. Oriented so that the sun's first rays at the Summer Solstice shone on its central altar, Stonehenge accurately predicted eclipses as long ago as 1900 to 1600 B.C.E. One theory suggests that Stonehenge served as the first planetarium. If the distances are calculated from the center of Stonehenge to the various rings of stones in the monument and multiplied by 10^{10}, they correspond to the distances of the planets (Mercury through Jupiter) from the sun.

Astrology was important to the ancient Maya, too, who cast birthcharts for male babies and calculated a solar calendar consisting of 365 days. The Caracol observatory at

Chichen Itza, Mexico, demonstrates the Mayan familiarity with astrological/astronomical cycles; its windows relate to the positions of the planets at different times of the year.

An advanced knowledge of astrology is also depicted in the medieval basilica of San Miniato al Monte in Florence. Occult and astrological symbolism can be found throughout the church and a large zodiac wheel constructed of colored marble adorns the floor of the nave. Interestingly, the sun is positioned in the middle of the zodiac circle, even though when the church was built the earth was believed to be at the center of our solar system.

During the Middle Ages and Renaissance, cathedrals were constructed by special guilds of tradesmen trained in the ancient mysteries. These secret brotherhoods of masons and workmen, who understood occult symbolism and the magick of mathematics, incorporated their knowledge into religious architecture, where it would be perceived intuitively by the uninitiated. (The Freemasons descended from this early mystery guild.)

Zodiac symbols and other astrological details are still featured in religious buildings throughout Europe, the British Isles, and North America. Undoubtedly, the architects understood the divine relationship between the heavenly bodies and life on earth. The elaborate rose windows in Notre Dame cathedral in Paris and in the cathedrals at Chartres, France, and Lausanne, Switzerland, for instance, contain astrological motifs. Even today, it's not uncommon to find zodiac images—particularly of the bull, lion, eagle, and human representing the four fixed signs, Taurus, Leo, Scorpio, and Aquarius, and the four New Testament gospels—in churches in this country, although most parishioners don't comprehend the connection and many church officials would probably discount their significance.

Astrology and the Body

Until a few hundred years ago, astrology and medicine were closely linked. The writings of Hermes Trismegistos, author of *The Emerald Tablet* and said to have been the first alchemist, proposed that the human body existed as a microcosm of the universe and linked various illnesses with the decanates (10-degree divisions) of the astrological signs. Hippocrates believed that "a physician without a knowledge of astrology has no right to call himself a physician." In his *Complete Herbal*, the 17th-century healer Nicholas Culpeper assigned astrological correspondences to medicinal plants. He also recommended gathering herbs during the days and hours ruled by the planets that were related to the illness being treated. (I discuss astrological-herbal connections in Chapter 7; planetary days and hours are covered in Chapter 9.)

In the 1930s, British bacteriologist Edward Bach revived the lost art of healing with flower remedies, a process that involves infusing the energetic properties of flowers into water. Plants are picked according to astrological influences and floated in water for several hours to allow the sun's rays to transfer the vibrational pattern from the flowers to the water, which is then ingested to heal specific emotional problems. According to Bach, one of the reasons flower remedies are so effective is that they combine the four elements—"the earth to nurture the plant, the air from which it feeds, the sun or fire to enable it to impart its powers, and water...to be enriched with its beneficent magnetic healing."

A. T. Mann, astrologer and practitioner of the energy diagnostic technique known as radionics, was probably the first person to notice a similarity between the patterns on Rae cards (used in radionics therapy to encourage vibrational healing) and the configuration of an astrological chart. By translating a patient's birthchart into the circles and lines of a Rae card, Mann could treat the patient with the energy of his or her own horoscope. Mann also demonstrated relationships between homeopathic remedies and the astrological signs.

For the last 25 years, Dr. Michelle Levan has studied the correlations between sun signs and certain illnesses. Aries people, she found, are most likely to suffer from head ailments and injuries. Tauruses contract throat and thyroid problems. Geminis are susceptible to conditions involving the nervous system. Cancers experience stomach troubles and ulcers. Leos are vulnerable to heart conditions and difficulties with the lower spine. Virgos have problems with the liver and/or elimination system. Libras are more likely to get kidney stones than people born under the other signs. The colon and generative organs are Scorpio's weak spot. Sagittarians tend to suffer with sciatica and diseases of the liver. Arthritis and gall bladder problems plague Capricorns. Aquarians have trouble with their circulatory systems, and Pisceans are susceptible to allergies, lymphatic difficulties, and foot ailments.

Levan's findings confirm Western medical astrology's associations between the different parts of the human body and the planets, houses, and signs. See Appendix A for the generally accepted correspondences between planets, signs, and parts of the body.

Astrology and Music

Since antiquity, music has played an important role in rituals, celebrations, and spiritual practice in virtually all cultures throughout the world. Music can induce trances and other altered states of consciousness; it soothes the psyche during meditation and stimulates aggression during battle.

The ancient Chaldeans, to whom we are indebted for much of the astrology we use today, linked the seven notes of the musical scale to the seven nearest bodies in our solar system, a correlation known as the "music of the spheres." Each of the heavenly bodies vibrates, or hums, a specific tone that is audible to sensitive individuals. The Greek mathematician Pythagoras also theorized about the music of the spheres, speculating that the distances between the earth, the sun, the moon, and the planets formed a universal harmony and produced an intense melody.

It is said that many of the greatest composers, including Mozart, Handel, Bach, and Beethoven, were attuned to this cosmic music, which may be why their compositions can uplift our spirits and promote body-mind healing.

As with most areas of astrology, authorities disagree about which notes relate to which planets and zodiac signs. For a system developed by Max Heindel, see Appendix B.

You could think of your birthchart as a musical composition in which planetary placements and relationships form chords, riffs, and rhythms that are either melodious or dissonant. Perhaps by listening to your natal song, you could balance your body's systems or gain insights into your purpose in life. What would your chart sound like if it were translated into music?

Astrology and Language

Even the letters and words we use to communicate with each other—and with the Creator—are linked to the heavenly bodies. In Kabbalah, Jewish mysticism, Hebrew's seven double letters are associated with the sun, moon, and the five planets nearest to earth. The 12 simple letters relate to the signs of the zodiac. Refer to Appendix C for a list of correspondences.

In the Druid alphabet, the consonants correspond to the signs of the zodiac, the vowels to the planets. The seven days of the week are also associated with the seven "original" heavenly bodies (sun, moon, Mercury, Venus, Mars, Jupiter), as well as seven trees that were sacred to the Druids. See Appendix D for a list of correspondences. There are also connections between astrology and the letters of the Greek and the Arabic alphabets; see appendices E and F, respectively.

Not much evidence is available about the relationship between astrology and English, perhaps because English is a newer system or because it is the language of business, rather than spiritual pursuits and magick.

Astrology and the Chakras

The body's seven major chakras, or vital energy centers according to Eastern traditions, are linked with the planets and luminaries. Chakra is a Sanskrit word meaning "wheel," and clairvoyants describe them as resembling rotating discs that run from the base of the spine to the top of the head. (Actually, they exist in the etheric body that surrounds and permeates the physical body.)

Not all sources and philosophies agree about which planets correspond to which chakras, however, and in some cases more than one planet influences a particular chakra. My opinion is that Saturn rules the root chakra, Pluto and Mars rule the sacral chakra, the moon and Jupiter rule the solar plexus chakra, the sun rules the heart chakra, Venus and Mercury rule the throat chakra, Uranus rules the brow chakra, and Neptune rules the crown chakra.

Body-workers, energy healers, and psychics often connect the seven colors of the visible spectrum with the seven chakras. For instructions on balancing and attuning these energy vortices by projecting colors and planetary symbols onto them, see Appendix G.

Chapter 2

What Is Magick?

"Every intentional act is a magical act."
—Aleister Crowley

In essence, magick is the process of consciously creating circumstances by manipulating energy. From the magician's point of view, there's no such thing as luck—we make our own "luck." Ceremonial magick, shamanism, creative visualization, ecstatic sex, chanting, and feng shui are all types of magick, and there are many others. Despite differences in their outer forms, all have one thing in common: they focus the magician's intent, strengthening his or her ability to direct natural energies in order to produce a desired effect. Will is the power behind magick—magick is willed action.

We live in a magickal universe of unlimited potential, a universe comprised of worlds seen and unseen, physical and nonphysical. These worlds are infinitely complex, but with the right tools and understanding, we can navigate them gracefully.

Magicians are people who are aware of the subtle energies that exist all around us and have learned to consciously tap these energies for specific purposes. They don't just perform a ritual or spell now and again, they are in constant contact with the forces of the cosmos and try to live in harmony with those forces. As Donald Michael Kraig, author of *Modern Magick*, says, "Magick is not something you do, magick is something you are."

Most of the time, we are only aware of the physical realm—and only a small part of that. Our vision is limited; so is our ability to shape our destinies. Through the use of magick, we can erase the barriers that normally restrict us and walk between the worlds. We can expand our perception to see nonphysical entities and subtle fields of energy. We can transcend time and look into the past and future. We can visit the stars or the center of the earth. Most importantly, we can create the lives we want for ourselves and help others to do the same.

Actually, we are creating our own realities all the time, whether we realize it or not. Many healers, for instance, believe that our bodies are formed not only by heredity, diet, exercise, and so on, but also by our attitudes and emotions. Therefore, we can alter physical conditions and cure illnesses by changing the way we think, feel, and experience life. The reason for this is that every condition exists in the astral and etheric realms—the subtle energy fields that surround and interpenetrate the physical realm—before it manifests physically. The Buddha taught that "we are what we think. All that we are arises with our thoughts. With our thoughts, we make the world." This is one of the premises on which the practice of magick is based.

The Power of Intent

Every action produces a reaction. Every thought, word, and deed causes repercussions, in much the same way a stone tossed into a pond creates ripples on the surface of the water. There is a Chinese saying that when a butterfly moves its wings, the wind currents on the opposite side of the world are affected.

In magickal work, the magician's intent is the most important part of any spell or ritual. Magickal tools, words, gestures, garments, and other accoutrements can enhance the work, but they don't generate the magick—they merely aid the magician by lending their energies to his or her purposes and by helping the magician to focus his or her intent.

Our thoughts and feelings are like seeds that, when projected into the universe, take root in the energetic matrix that links us with everything else in the cosmos and eventually grow into material forms. Therefore, one of the first and most important skills we must learn is disciplining our minds. Random, careless thoughts and idle statements can affect us as well as others. The more focused and impassioned our thoughts and words are, the more power they have.

When we utter angry oaths or dwell on hurtful thoughts, those energies become part of the cosmic vibrational pattern. Depending on circumstances, these energies may cause harm to ourselves or someone else, or combine with collective disruptive energies to produce war, earthquakes, or various forms of violent activity. Indeed, much so-called "black" magick is performed by people who don't realize what they're doing.

By projecting loving, joyful, peaceful thoughts into our energetic environment, we can heal ourselves and our planet. Botanist Luther Burbank demonstrated that positive thoughts helped plants grow stronger and healthier and even alter their usual characteristics. The work of Larry Dossey, M.D., presents convincing evidence that prayer—which is essentially targeted, positive thought—can reverse even life-threatening illnesses. Interestingly, it works even if the recipient of the prayers doesn't know about it. Thus, prayer can be considered a type of magick.

Sometimes, though, even well-meaning intentions may be incorrect in a particular situation. Perhaps we believe what we are doing is helpful or in the best interests of ourselves or another person. It's natural to want to come to the aid of someone who is experiencing difficulty—a physical illness, financial problems, a broken heart. However, there are usually reasons for the difficulties we face, and life's challenges are often learning opportunities in disguise. For example, a butterfly must struggle and fight its way out of the cocoon in order to strengthen its wings so it can fly.

Because we might not know the underlying reasons that a particular difficulty has presented itself, we should not attempt to do magick for another person unless he or she requests our help. Even then, we should ask that person's higher self if our assistance is appropriate before we act. Or, consult an oracle such as the *I Ching*, runes, or tarot to gain insight into the matter and advice about how to proceed. The same holds true when we do magick for ourselves. The best way to ensure that whatever we do is in accord with the circumstances, time, karmic situations, unconscious needs, and other conditions is to always begin and/or end all magickal operations with a statement such as, "Let this be done if it is in harmony with Divine Will, my (or another person's) own true will, and for the good of all concerned."

Magick Isn't Black and White

Magick has gotten a bad rap over the past few millennia. Religious zealots and other misguided, and sometimes self-serving, individuals and power groups have imprisoned, tortured, murdered, and otherwise persecuted untold numbers of magicians, astrologers, witches, and people accused (rightly or falsely) of practicing the occult arts. During a reign of terror sometimes called the Burning Times, which lasted from the 15th through the 18th centuries, at least tens of thousands and perhaps millions (depending on which source you choose to believe) of people in Europe and North America were put to death in horrible ways for supposedly doing magick. Most of them were women and girls. (By the way, the word "occult" simply means "hidden." To avoid persecution, magickal practitioners were forced into hiding, hence the label. Even today many magicians must keep their beliefs and work secret from coworkers, neighbors, and loved ones.)

Magick isn't inherently good or bad, black or white. Magick is the utilization of natural energy. It is like electricity, which can be used to light our homes or to kill people, but which itself is neither good nor bad. Because we are familiar with electricity and its properties, we respect its power and use it sensibly, instead of fearing it. Most people, however, are ignorant about magick and tend to be afraid of what they don't understand.

In actuality, magicians are less likely to do harm than ordinary people because they are aware of the potential ramifications of their actions. Once we realize that our thoughts have power and that we are integrally connected to everything else in the web of life, it becomes imperative that we use our power responsibly. It is foolish to do otherwise.

Donald Michael Kraig, in his book *Modern Sex Magick*, sums it up this way: "We are part of a mind-body-spirit-environment matrix that unites us with our neighbors, our loved ones, our land, our world, our universe and the Divine. When we can accept that we are part of that matrix, we will intrinsically realize that to cheat or hurt our neighbors or land also cheats and hurts us. To treat everyone and everything with respect and honor is simply a way of respecting and honoring ourselves."

Magick Isn't a Parlor Game

We must be still if we wish to perceive the subtle vibrations of the earth and sky, sense the currents in this world and beyond, and use them for magickal purposes. Focus and clarity are essential in doing magick. Just as static in the atmosphere interrupts radio transmission, mental static interferes with the smooth flow of magickal intent. Being quiet also means turning off the TV, radio, and stereo periodically and spending time alone. As the Sufi mystic/poet Rumi wrote, "Silence is the sea, and speech is like the river. The sea is seeking you: don't seek the river."

Working safely and effectively with the forces of the universe requires a firm grounding in the physical realm, emotional balance, mental clarity, and pure motives. Magicians and astrologers, therefore, must discipline themselves psychologically and physically, in order to open the doors of perception and to avoid doing harm to themselves or others. Daily meditation, yoga, periods of enforced silence, and other such practices help us center ourselves so we can receive guidance from higher sources and hear the "still, small voice within." Rudolf Steiner's *How to Know Higher Worlds* (previously titled *Knowledge of the Higher Worlds and Its Attainment*) also offers a good course to follow.

Sincerity, too, is essential. The *I Ching* reminds us that attitudes of suspicion and mistrust prevent the Sage from relating to us and that unless we are wholly directed toward what is true and good he won't be able to respond to us. The same is true of your magickal powers and your ability to use hidden forces successfully.

Magick is not a parlor game. Like astrology, magickal proficiency requires many years of dedicated study and practice—a little magick can be a dangerous thing. Nor is magick a weapon to wield for vengeful, manipulative, or greedy purposes. The temptation to misuse power when you have it is often difficult to resist, but the consequences of doing so are great. One of the fundamental laws of magick is that every action produces an energetic reaction, and whatever energy you put out returns to you in kind, sometimes threefold.

Discovering the Magician in You

We all possess magickal powers and are capable of shaping our world. One of the wonderful things about magickal ability is that it doesn't discriminate—you can be any age, sex, race, size, physical condition, or income bracket. An open mind and a desire to take charge of your own life are the only prerequisites for learning magick. As with any other skill, some people are more naturally talented than others. But also as with any other skill, magickal ability improves with practice.

A thought or vision always precedes physical manifestation. Just as the idea of a building must exist in the architect's mind before it can take physical form, so must a concept of what you want to create live in your imagination before it can materialize. Clear, vivid ideas tend to produce better results than nebulous or conflicted ones. Additionally, the more energy you can imbue your thoughts with the more power they'll have.

Magick isn't only a matter of using your head, however—it involves the heart, intuition, and senses as well. Becoming a magician means learning to balance and unite these seemingly disparate parts of yourself, so that they work in concert. It means honoring their wisdom and listening to what they have to tell you. It means being aware of your body-mind-spirit nature and getting in touch with yourself at a deep level. If your subconscious desires and your conscious objectives aren't in sync, your magickal results may be less than satisfactory.

With experience, you'll discover what works best for you. The study and practice of magick are probably infinite in scope—there is always more to learn. As you develop your abilities and continue your magickal work, your approach, focus, and expression will probably change. In the beginning, however, here are a few tips that I hope will be helpful.

You'll see it when you believe it

Unless you are open to the possibility that magick is real and that you can use it to enhance your own life, you probably won't be very successful. Of course, people often perform magickal acts without realizing they are doing so, but usually this type of unintentional magick is scattered, distorted, or relatively ineffective. Working magick requires trust—in yourself and the universe—as well as an open mind that's willing to receive wisdom and guidance, from both your own inner knowing and the Divine.

Do it and let it go

You must also believe that your magick will work. Doubt and questioning can undo the effects of a spell. Once you've cast a spell, trust that it is already working and that all will be well. Then stop thinking about it. Don't wonder if you did it "right" or become discouraged if the desired effect doesn't occur as quickly as you'd like. Things happen when they're supposed to happen, and magickal time isn't necessarily the same as ordinary time.

Distance is irrelevant in magick

Because magick isn't subject to the physical limitations of time and space, you can do magick in Boston and produce an effect in Tokyo. Many magicians perform long-distance healing, for example. Thoughts, visions, and intentions are transmitted instantaneously, so it doesn't matter if the person you're communicating with is next door or on the other side of the world. Distance is also irrelevant in astrology. In fact, most people experience the energetic impact of far-away Pluto as being much stronger than that of our neighbor Venus.

Awareness is important to magickal work

As I stated earlier, we exist in an energetic web that involves all of creation. The more aware you are of everything else within this web—entities, currents, vibrations, and so on—the more effectively you can work with them. Nurture your sensitivity to the environment around you as well as to your own internal environment. Pay attention to your hunches and feelings. Watch for signals from your personal guides. Attune yourself to the energies of the people, creatures, and other living things that coexist on the planet with you. Learn to recognize and appreciate patterns in the universe.

Time of day may be a factor

Some of us are morning people, others are night people. Therefore, you'll probably find that there are certain times of the day or night when you can do your best magick. Usually you'll be more effective if you work magick when you're feeling rested and energized, rather than when you're tired (although many people report that doing magick revitalizes them). You may also discover that your magickal abilities are more powerful at particular times of the week, month, or year. Pay attention to your own natural rhythms and respect them.

Play to your strengths

We all have special, unique skills and talents that we can utilize in our magick work. Your astrological makeup, as well as your personal interests, training, and life experiences will also be factors in the type of magick you're drawn to and the way you use your magickal abilities. Artists, for instance, are often good magicians because they are adept at creating vivid images in their minds. Actors may be wonderful at leading rituals. Gardeners, not surprisingly, often gravitate toward herbal and plant magick. People who enjoy systems and order might excel at ritual magick.

Two heads may be better than one

Working with a partner or group can be advantageous, as long as the other people have relatively similar views, expectations, and intentions. Some people enjoy doing magick in couples or groups that include both sexes in order to balance the male-female energetic polarity. Many individuals find their own energy is strengthened when it's combined with the energy of other magicians and that the power generated by two or more people working together is multiplicative; in other words, the whole is greater than the sum of its parts. Another advantage of working with other people is you can share ideas, techniques, and experiences, thus improving everyone's magickal knowledge.

Keep a grimoire

This is a journal of your magickal work and experiences. Here you can record spells, practices, results, your thoughts and impressions, and so on. Your grimoire is both a collection of magickal information and a tool for self-discovery. Just as keeping a dream journal helps you discern patterns in your psycho-spiritual development as an individual, keeping a grimoire enables you to chart and understand your own cycles, abilities, inner wisdom, and growth as a magician.

Practice makes perfect

Magickal work, like everything else in life, requires practice. Dedication and diligence pay off. The more you put into it, the more you'll get out of it. And the more you do it, the better you'll become.

Chapter 3

Birthchart Basics

"Studying astrology can bring the higher perceptions that life requires."

—Robert Hand

Astrology is a vast and complex field, far too extensive to cover in its entirety here or in any one book. For those of you not already familiar with astrology, the basics provided here will help you work with celestial energies to understand personality (through the natal chart) and predict future events (through the use of transits, progressions, solar return charts, and other techniques). You will also gain an understanding of the complex relationship between the heavenly bodies and life here on earth. A good working knowledge of the celestial energies and your own birthchart can be invaluable in magickal practice.

The Planets

The planets make things happen in a chart. They provide the energy, the impetus, the action. Think of the planets as actors on a stage, carrying out the drama of life.

For convenience, astrologers often refer to the sun and moon as "planets," even though they are not. We also speak of the sun's "movement" through the birthchart, although the sun, of course, does not actually move. In geocentric (earth-centered) astrology—which is what most modern Western astrologers use—we are concerned with how the heavenly bodies affect life here on earth; therefore, the earth is viewed as the center. The other members of our solar system are interpreted according to how they appear to us from earth.

The planets and their energies are discussed in Chapter 4, so I'll only give keywords here. My book *Planets in Signs* provides more extensive information about these heavenly bodies.

Sun: Identity, self-expression, conscious personality, your role in the present lifetime.

Moon: Emotions, the subconscious, home and family matters, the past.

Mercury: Communication, mental orientation, short trips.

Venus: Relationships, love, creativity, money, women.

Mars: Assertiveness, action, physical energy, desires, men.

Jupiter: Expansion, good luck, long-distance travel, higher knowledge.

Saturn: Limitation, responsibility, work, stability, tests.

Uranus: Change, unexpected events, anything unconventional.

Neptune: Spirituality, illusion, imagination, dissolution, sacrifice.

Pluto: Transformation, power, obsession, fears.

Houses

The 12 houses represent areas of life experience where the action takes place. Think of the houses as the stages on which the planets perform. The planet(s) and sign(s) in a house show what sort of energy is focused into a particular area of your life and how you express the issues associated with that house.

Here are brief descriptions of the areas of life associated with each house. Dane Rudhyar's *The Astrological Houses* and Rob Hand's *Horoscope Symbols* offer valuable insights into these sectors of the birthchart.

1st house: Physical appearance, personality, the image you project, how you appear to other people initially.

2nd house: Material/financial resources, talents and abilities with which you can earn money, values, sexuality.

3rd house: Relationships with siblings and neighbors, communication, early education.

4th house: Your sense of security, early childhood, heritage, relationships with parents, home and family matters.

5th house: Self-expression, creativity, children, love affairs, entertainment, where you invest your love.

6th house: Work, service, work relationships, health (especially as it relates to work).

7th house: Marriage or long-term romantic relationships, business partnerships, other contractual one-to-one relationships.

8th house: A partner's resources, other people's money (such as loans and inheritances), occult knowledge, death and rebirth.

9th house: Higher education, religion, long-distance travel, publishing and widespread communication, foreign cultures.

10th house: Public image, career, social position or status.

11th house: Group activities, professional organizations, goals and objectives, friends, things that encourage and validate you.

12th house: The subconscious, latent talents, secrets, endings, unacknowledged parts of yourself.

A house that contains many planets is a sphere of life that's very important to you, where lots of action is likely to occur. If you have Venus, Mars, and Jupiter in the fifth house, for example, you may have many love affairs and/or be very creative. An empty, or "void," house is one that may not be of central importance to you in this lifetime, though it does not mean that part of your life is missing. A void seventh house, for example, doesn't mean you'll never marry, only that marriage isn't necessarily a principal focus for your development in this incarnation.

Angles

An astrological chart is partitioned into quadrants by angles known as the ascendant and descendant (the cusps of the first and seventh houses respectively), the midheaven (the cusp of the 10th house), and the imum colei (the cusp of the fourth house). Planetary contacts with these angles are important in natal and predictive astrology.

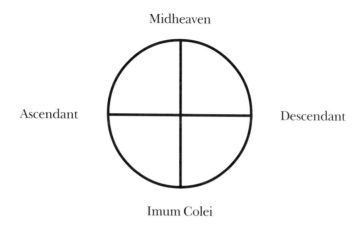

(Figure 3.1)

Signs

The 12 signs of the zodiac color the energies and actions of the planets. You could think of the signs as the costumes the actors (planets) wear. The signs are represented by a band of constellations through which the planets appear to move when we look at them from the earth. At one time, the actual constellations lined up with the signs which bear their names and the sun was positioned at 0 degrees Aries on the first day of spring. However, this is no longer true due to a "wobble" in the earth's motion, which each year shifts our position very slightly in relation to the sun's position against the backdrop of these constellations. Skeptics sometimes use this point to attempt to discredit astrology's validity, but most Western astrologers find that this shift does not really alter the meanings of the signs. (See Chapter 5 for more information about the signs. My book *Planets in Signs* provides in-depth interpretations of the sun, moon, and planets through all 12 signs of the zodiac.)

Planetary Aspects

Aspects are angular relationships between planets or between planets and sensitive points in the 360-degree circle that comprises an astrological chart. Think of aspects as energetic connections between planets or points in an astrological chart. When two or more heavenly bodies are in aspect to each other, they influence each other's expression. The closer the aspect is to "exact," the stronger the relationship is between the planets involved. Aspects may exist between planets at the time of someone's birth (in which case they affect the person throughout his or her entire life). Aspects are also created temporarily during what's known as a transit, when a planet's orbital motion brings it into a position where it forms a connection with the birth position of a planet or angle. A birthchart that contains many planetary aspects indicates a complex personality. The most important aspects are:

Conjunction: Two or more bodies positioned within about 7 degrees of each other in the chart. This is generally considered to be the strongest aspect and it may be favorable or difficult, depending on the planets involved. Conjunct (or conjoined) planets operate in tandem.

Sextile: Two or more planets positioned approximately 54 to 66 degrees apart. This is a harmonious aspect and the planets involved support each other's expression.

Square: Two or more planets positioned approximately 83 to 97 degrees apart. This stressful aspect indicates tension between the planets involved. Some sort of action is often prompted by the square in order to alleviate the tension.

Trine: Two or more planets positioned approximately 113 to 127 degrees apart. This is considered the most harmonious aspect. The planets involved enhance each other's energies and promote ease of expression.

Inconjunct/
  Quincunx: Two or more planets positioned approximately 147 to 153 degrees apart. This stressful aspect suggests difficulty integrating the energies of the planets involved.

Opposition: Two or more planets positioned approximately 173 to 180 degrees apart. This challenging aspect produces stress between the planets involved, often resulting in projection or an inability to integrate two facets of personality.

Chapter 4

Planets, Elements, and Their Magick

"There are more things in heaven and earth, Horatio, than are dreamt of in your philosophy."
—Shakespeare, *Hamlet*

Astrologers believe the heavenly bodies and their movements through the sky influence everything that happens here on earth. Some of these influences are readily apparent—it's easy to see how the earth's changing relationship to the sun creates the different seasons and how the moon's phases affect the tides. Mercury's retrograde cycles, when the planet appears to be moving backward in the sky, often cause communication difficulties, delays, problems with computers, and mix-ups in general. The actions of the other planets may be less obvious to the untrained eye, but they are nonetheless significant. For example, Pluto's entrance into Sagittarius in the mid-1990s led to the creation of the Internet.

Each planet possesses a unique, distinctive energy and plays a special role in the cosmic plan. We respond to these energies inwardly and outwardly, even if we don't always recognize that we're doing it. Once you become familiar with planetary energies, however, you can use them to enhance your magickal work and facilitate personal growth. By tracking the planet's cycles through the heavens, you can predict events in your own life and in the outer world.

The Planets

Below are basic descriptions of the heavenly bodies in our solar system, how they affect us here on earth, and the types of magick in which each can be best utilized. (My book *Planets in Signs* discusses the planets and luminaries in greater detail. In Chapter 7, you'll learn about the connections between celestial powers and the natural world. Chapter 9 explains the importance of astrological timing in spellworking. Chapter 12 describes how astrologers make predictions based on planetary movements.)

The Sun

Everything in our solar system revolves around the sun—without the sun, life as we know it here on earth would cease to exist. From an astrological perspective, the sun is the supreme figure in a birthchart, the primary indicator of an individual's personality, sense of self, identity, and mode of expression in the world. I like to think of the sun as the symbol of the "present you," the person you are right now, in this lifetime. In the birthchart, it also shows your role in this incarnation, how you envision yourself, what you aspire to be and achieve.

The sun's energy—astrologically as well as physically—is usually felt to be life-enhancing, vitalizing, beneficial, and uplifting. For the most part, we are comfortable with the qualities and characteristics associated with our sun signs. If you meet someone whose sun makes a favorable connection with your birthchart, you'll probably feel positively disposed toward that person; he or she will tend to bring out the best in you.

As the earth orbits the sun, solar energy illuminates different parts of your birthchart and activates certain areas of your life. I've noticed, for example, that I often begin new jobs or important projects in February and March, when the sun moves through the tenth house of my birthchart—the sector associated with career.

In magickal work

Because the sun's vibration is outgoing, invigorating, active, and expansive, it can augment magick that involves growth, self-expression, and most outer-world activities. Solar energy is usually considered positive, an asset in nearly any endeavor. Tap this celestial power to help you get a job, increase your prosperity, improve your image, spark your creativity, aid business ventures, or strengthen your physical condition. If your intention is to encourage growth, perform magick between the Winter Solstice and the Summer Solstice, when the sun's light is increasing.

The Moon

In our solar system, the moon reflects the sun's light, shining only through its interaction with another luminary. This is an apt image for the moon's role in astrology, for this celestial body is associated with close personal relationships and family ties. If you meet someone whose moon forms a harmonious connection with your own, you'll probably feel a positive emotional and/or intuitive link with that person. Someone whose sun is in the same sign as your moon may illuminate your inner self, complementing and fulfilling you.

The moon also symbolizes the past—your early childhood experiences, your heritage, your previous incarnations and karma. Its placement in your birthchart shows how you give and receive nurturing as well as what makes you feel secure and comfortable. The moon also influences your physical body, which is a product of both nature and nurture.

Emotions, intuition, instincts, and the unconscious are governed by the moon. As the moon travels through the 12 signs of the zodiac every 28 days, it briefly highlights the different parts of your birthchart in the process, triggering emotional responses to people and situations in your life.

In magickal work

Because the moon is connected with emotions and intuition, its energy is fundamental to the practice of magick. The symbol of the archetypal feminine, this celestial power is honored by goddess-oriented spiritual traditions. Tap lunar energy to work magick that involves love relationships, home and family matters, fertility/pregnancy, health issues, security/protection, divination, and intuition, or to strengthen your feminine side (regardless of your sex). The moon also rules the natural world, which is why its cycles are important in farming and animal husbandry.

However, lunar phases can be utilized in virtually any type of magickal work. The new moon is a time of beginnings. As the moon starts to wax, initiate new endeavors and plant seeds that you want to grow. This is the best time to do prosperity or fertility magick, to launch a business or begin a relationship. Create talismans to attract love, money, or whatever you want while the moon is waxing. The full moon marks a period of completion, when developing matters come to fruition. During the waning moon, do magick that involves decrease or letting go. Create amulets to block unwanted energies while the moon is waning. The last three days before the new moon are good times to break old bonds or eliminate unwanted habits.

Each month, for a few minutes or for as long as a couple days, the moon is said to be "void of course" which means the period between the time it makes its last aspect to another heavenly body while it is in a particular sign until the moon moves into the next sign. (You'll have to check an ephemeris to determine when these periods are in effect.)

Things begun during these disjointed periods of astrological "limbo" are unlikely to come to fruition—this is not a favorable time to perform magick!

Eclipses are particularly powerful celestial events, and they can be either advantageous or disadvantageous for working magick. Generally, solar eclipses favor lunar practices and moon-related magick; lunar eclipses support solar activities and sun-oriented magick. Eclipses often act as catalysts, prompting actions or awarenesses. If you begin something during an eclipse, you will witness further developments related to it with each subsequent eclipse. (In her book *The Eagle and the Lark*, Bernadette Brady discusses eclipse cycles in depth and interprets the specific meanings of each eclipse.)

Mercury

In mythology, Mercury was the messenger of the gods. In astrology, this planet's role is similar: it rules communication, thinking and many mental processes, and short trips. Mercury's position in your birthchart shows how you acquire and process information, how you exchange ideas with others, and your attitude toward intelligence and language (but not how smart you are). Because communication and transportation are key ingredients in business, Mercury is also associated with commerce. Mercury rules the hands and is an indicator of manual as well as verbal dexterity.

If you meet someone who has Mercury in the same sign as you do, the two of you will "speak the same language." In most instances, you should be able to communicate well with someone whose sun is in the same sign as your Mercury. Mercury's passage through your birthchart may stimulate periods of learning, travel, or sharing ideas and information either verbally or in writing.

In magickal work

Because Mercury rules speech and thinking, it is involved in most magickal work. You tap Mercury's energy whenever you use affirmations, incantations, sigils, hand gestures, or consciously created thought-forms. If you are doing magick that involves travel, communication, job-hunting, business deals, or contracts and negotiations, this planet's energy can be particularly beneficial.

Every four months or so, for approximately three weeks, Mercury goes retrograde. During these periods, the planet appears to be moving backward in its orbit around the sun. Mercury's retrograde cycles can cause confusion, mistakes, delays, and difficulties with communication (and communication equipment). Obviously, these are not ideal times to do magick—your objectives may not be clear; you might not formulate or communicate your intentions accurately; you could make mistakes or run into unforeseen complications. Sometimes spells don't work out as you'd planned or results take longer than you'd expected.

On the positive side, retrograde periods can be advantageous for finding lost objects or reconnecting with people you haven't seen in a while. These are also good times to develop your intuitive processes, nurture your emotional/feeling side, go on a spiritual retreat or vision quest, or do past-life work.

Venus

Venus was the Roman goddess of love and beauty; these are the areas the planet presides over in astrology, too. Along with the moon, it symbolizes feminine energy. In a man's birthchart, Venus represents his ideal lover; in a woman's chart, the planet describes her image of herself and her own femininity. Venus governs relationships of all kinds, but especially romantic ones. Its position in the birthchart shows how you give and receive love, what you want and value in relationships, and how you attract other people to you.

Someone whose Venus makes a positive contact with your Venus is likely to engender affectionate feelings in you. Strong astrological connections involving this planet usually exist between lovers and spouses, but they are also important in business partnerships because Venus promotes harmony, cooperation, and ease. Relationships are affected—usually for the better—when Venus cycles highlight your chart.

This planet also rules the arts and it is usually prominent in the charts of creative people. Its movement through the birthchart inspires imagination, creative output, and an appreciation of the good things in life. Venus is linked with money and resources, too, and can have a positive impact on your finances. Considered a "benefic" by astrologers, Venus focuses good vibrations into any area it touches, bathing that part of your life in a rosy glow. However, it has an indulgent, vain, and lazy side, so extravagance can be a problem when working with this planetary energy.

In magickal work

Not surprisingly, Venusian energy is a principal force behind love spells and sex magick. Venus also lends its power to magick involving relationships of all kinds, professional as well as personal. This planet can help you make a favorable impression on other people and attract individuals who benefit you socially and/or financially—tap its energy if you are looking for a job or support for a business venture, or when you're doing prosperity magick. When Venus is retrograde, however, confusion, mix-ups, reversals, and/or delays may occur in situations involving love or money. (Check an ephemeris for the dates when these cycles are in effect.)

Mars

Like the Roman war god it was named for, the planet Mars is connected with aggression, competition, and vitality. Its dynamic force can express negatively as anger, violence, selfishness, and cruelty, or positively as independence, assertiveness, strength, and bravery. Mars symbolizes the archetypal male energy in the cosmos. In a man's chart, it describes his image of his own masculinity; in a woman's chart, Mars represents her ideal man. Your desires are indicated by Mars and its position in the birthchart suggests how you go after what you want in life. Also associated with sex, it shows how you express sexuality as well as what excites you.

If you meet someone whose Mars contacts planets in your chart, you'll probably find the person stimulating. Whether this stimulation is experienced as energizing or stressful, motivating or annoying depends on the connection. Strong Mars links are often found between the charts of lovers, sparking a powerful sexual attraction, but they also turn up in enemies' charts.

Martian energy can bolster your self-confidence, prompting you to take action, be decisive, assert yourself, and face up to fears. Tap this planetary force when you need extra vitality or courage. Mars is often prominent in the charts of athletes, and its raw power can be an asset in many physical activities. However, this planet also has an impulsive, disruptive, arrogant side that can sometimes produce accidents or conflicts.

In magickal work

Mars gets involved in sex magick and in love spells when sexual passion is a key component in the relationship. Tap this planet's fearless, forceful nature when confronting dangerous situations, adversaries, challenges, or obstacles. If you need extra energy or inner strength, Mars can be an asset.

This planet often aids sexual problems resulting from diminished libido, exhaustion, poor self image, fear, or aging (especially in men). However, be careful using it in healing work as it can exacerbate some conditions rather than alleviating them.

Jupiter

The largest planet in our solar system, Jupiter is associated with growth and increase. It knows no bounds and expands whatever it touches, both physically and psychologically. Jupiter's domain includes higher knowledge and education, religion, philosophy, and long-distance travel—all of which expand our horizons and our understanding of the world. This planet's position in the birthchart shows where you are expansive, generous, unwilling to be restrained or prudent.

Sometimes called the "greater benefic," Jupiter's influence is generally considered positive and life-enhancing. As it travels through your birthchart, it prompts opportunities, good luck, and growth in the various areas of your life. When you meet someone whose Jupiter contacts one of your personal planets, you usually experience feelings of optimism. This person is someone you can have fun with and s/he may bring out the best in you by encouraging you to reach greater heights, increasing your self-esteem, or assisting you professionally, personally, spiritually, and/or financially.

Tap Jupiter's energy to help you improve your finances, make a good impression on other people, enhance your public image, advance professionally, or heighten your vitality. Like all the planets, though, Jupiter has a downside—it is indulgent, excessive, idealistic, and can lead you to overextend yourself physically or financially.

In magickal work

Jupiter promotes increase, so its energy can be useful when you are working magick that involves growth. Prosperity magick, love spells, blessings to attract success in a business/career venture or legal matter, and most healing work can be enhanced by Jupiter's fortunate vibrations.

Saturn

Saturn gets a lot of bad press from astrologers who connect it with karmic lessons, hardship, duty, and limitations. Indeed, Saturn is the taskmaster of the solar system—its job is to force us to discipline ourselves and accept responsibility. In contrast to expansive Jupiter, Saturn places restrictions on whatever it touches. Its position in your birthchart shows where you may undergo difficulties, feel inadequate, or be required to work hard for what you get. However, Saturn also brings valuable learning experiences, enabling you to grow and develop strengths through your own efforts. Despite Saturn's unsavory reputation, this planet doesn't actually cause problems—it merely brings us what we deserve and shows us the results of our actions, which is why it's connected with fate and karma.

As Saturn moves through your birthchart, you often encounter obstacles and tests, which may involve work, losses, restraint, self-reliance, and/or facing reality. If you meet someone whose Saturn makes a stressful connection with a planet in your chart, you'll probably view that person as demanding, unloving, or limiting to you in some way. On the positive side, this person may provide security or stability for you.

Saturn can be advantageous in practical matters or where order and pragmatism are needed. Tap its energy when you are laying foundations in business, financial, or personal situations. This planet can also help you build structures, set limits, get organized, plan for the future, create goals, or ground yourself in the material realm.

In magickal work

Because Saturn is associated with endings, it can be an asset in banishing rituals or when you need to let go of something. Its power is also useful in protection spells and can help you bind an enemy, establish boundaries, or build inner strength. The Winter Solstice is a good time to work with Saturn's energy.

Uranus

The planet of change, Uranus breaks down the structures and barriers Saturn erects. Its job is to shake up the status quo and usher in a new order. Astrologers connect it with anything that's unexpected or unconventional, as well as with electricity, modern technology, ingenuity, freedom, equality, and astrology. Uranus is the first of the outer planets, which are more concerned with cosmic and universal conditions than personal ones. Therefore, it is nearly impossible to control Uranus' energy—all we can do is guide our responses to its effect in our lives.

As Uranus travels through your birthchart, it sparks sudden changes and awarenesses in the different areas of your life. Sometimes it merely shakes up situations that have grown static and lets you look at things in a new light. Other times it shatters old patterns, conditions, and ideas irreparably. You usually feel stimulated and awakened by someone whose Uranus connects with the personal planets in your birthchart. Whether this is felt as exciting and inspiring or upsetting and stressful depends on the planets (and the people) involved. It's hard to predict the ramifications of a Uranus contact, but one thing is certain: you won't be the same after the experience.

Uranus often acts as a catalyst to action, pushing you to make necessary changes in your life. Tap its energy when you want to get out of a rut, be inventive or daring, stand up to authority, break through boundaries, or seek higher truths.

In magickal work

Uranus' energy can help you create change—but you might not be able to control how that change occurs or what the outcome will be. This planet is powerful and its force is often destructive. (It corresponds to The Tower in the tarot.) Uranus can also be an asset when you are working in the higher realms because it serves as a link to the astral world.

Neptune

Neptune rules the collective unconscious, the spiritual realms, and the nonphysical dimensions of existence. Astrologers connect it with dreams, fantasies, imagination, religion, compassion, intuition, and ideals. Its nature is to dissolve whatever it touches—not in a radically destructive way, like Uranus and Pluto do, but very subtly like water gradually eroding a rock.

This planet's movement through your birthchart heightens your sensitivity to the spiritual plane as well as to the world around you. It breaks down ego structures and attachments to material things, encouraging you to merge with the Divine. Artists, poets, and musicians often benefit from the imagination and insights Neptune inspires, which may prompt great outpourings of creative work. If you meet someone whose Neptune connects with a personal planet in your birthchart, s/he may inspire romantic or mystical feelings in you. However, Neptune produces confusion and idealistic yearnings, so you probably won't be able to see this person clearly.

Like the other outer planets, it functions on a transpersonal level and is concerned with universal conditions rather than individual ones. Its energy can help you become more creative, enhance your intuition, and enable you to connect with the spiritual realms. Because Neptune's influence is so elusive, it is very difficult to direct or control, sometimes resulting in delusions or self-destructive attitudes/behavior.

In magickal work

Neptune can aid psychic work and divination, strengthening your intuitive abilities, your sensitivity to other people, and your connection with the nonphysical worlds. The biggest challenge when tapping this planet's energy is interpreting your visions and impressions clearly, for Neptune's influence can produce illusions and confusion.

Pluto

Lord of the Underworld, Pluto rules things that are hidden from view. Secrets, the occult, illicit or clandestine activities, the inner dimensions of the psyche, taboos, sex, our deepest fears and obsessions fall into Pluto's domain. Also known as the destroyer, Pluto is connected with death and rebirth, and with transformations of all kinds.

As this planet travels through the birthchart, it forces us to confront our dark sides in order to transform the inner "beast" into "beauty." The process, however, is often quite painful for it requires us to let go of the things we cling to most tightly. Because Pluto's influence affects us at a deep level, we don't always comprehend what's happening to us or why—and we certainly can't control it. If you meet someone whose Pluto contacts one of the personal planets in your birthchart, that person is likely to transform you in some way—for good or ill—and might bring out the best or the worst in you. You may feel strongly drawn to this individual or repelled by him/her, and your feelings may be quite intense. Power struggles and control issues are often linked with Pluto contacts, as are passionate sexual attractions.

Like Uranus and Neptune, Pluto operates on a universal and karmic level with little regard for individual matters. Its role is to foster the evolution of all things, including humankind. Pluto's power can help you overcome obstacles, eliminate unwanted habits, attitudes, and behaviors, or connect with your inner self and the higher realms.

In magickal work

Astrologers consider Pluto to be the planetary ruler of magick, alchemy, and the occult in general. Whenever you do magick, you access invisible forces in the cosmos and in your own psyche to produce change. Although you can tap Pluto's energy to augment virtually any type of magickal work, it is especially useful in sex magick, in banishing and purification spells, to bind an enemy, to strengthen your inner power, or to transcend the physical realm and journey to other dimensions. Shapeshifting (the art of changing one's form to that of another being) and many shamanic practices also utilize Pluto's energy. Samhain is a good time to work with Pluto.

The Four Elements

Our world is comprised of four fundamental energies, or "elements," which are the building blocks of life. When astrologers speak of the elements, they aren't referring to the scientific table of elements, they mean the archetypal modes of experience that are inherent in all things. Although these four elements—fire, earth, air, and water—do exist physically, for the purposes of this book I am more concerned with their vibrational natures than their material ones.

From the magician's point of view, everything resonates with the energetic patterning of one or more of the elements. We humans are composites of the elemental energies contained in our birthcharts.

The four elements are essential ingredients in astrology and in the tarot, where they are depicted as the four suits. They are also linked with the four directions: North/earth, East/air, South/fire, West/water. In medieval medicine we see representations of these elements in the four humors, and in Jungian psychology they appear as the four character types (intuitive, sensation, thinking, and feeling). Some people associate the four Christian gospels and Buddhism's Four Noble Truths with the four elements.

According to astrologer Stephen Arroyo, "The four elements are not merely 'symbols' or abstract concepts, but rather they refer to the vital forces that make up the entire creation that can be perceived by the physical senses.... The elements are therefore not only the foundation of astrology and all occult sciences, but they comprise everything we can normally perceive and experience."

Because magicians are concerned with shaping the forces of the cosmos in order to create particular results, they are very much in tune with the four elements and understand how these energies operate in both the physical and non-physical realms. During rituals, a magician may petition the guardians or angels of the elements for protection and/or assistance. Magickal tools are also linked with the elements, as you'll see in Chapter 10.

Before you can use either astrology or magick effectively, you'll need to become familiar with the elements and their essential natures. The basic qualities of each element are given below, but I recommend reading Stephen Arroyo's *Astrology, Psychology, and the Four Elements* to gain a deeper knowledge of how these forces operate in our lives and in the universe.

Fire

We can begin to understand the essence of the fire element if we look at its celestial counterpart, the sun. This heavenly body provides the life-giving warmth and light we need to survive on earth. Without the sun's fiery energy, nothing on our planet would thrive. In an esoteric sense, fire represents the creative spirit that enlivens form, initiates action, and sparks imagination. Author Kelynda calls fire "the life force that drives all things to grow, flower, reproduce, and die."

Active, outer-directed, and dynamic, fire symbolizes the raw, undiluted masculine or yang power present in the cosmos. In astrology, this element contains the zodiac signs Aries, Leo, and Sagittarius. In the tarot, the fire element is represented by the suit of wands. The colors red and orange embody the fire element. In feng shui, loud noises, straight lines, and rapid movement are linked with fire. The fire element underlies combat, sports, sexual passion, artistic inspiration, and acts of courage. People with an abundance of fire energy in their birthcharts are assertive, daring, independent, self-centered, outgoing, optimistic, impractical, and visionary.

Fire Magick

Fire magick is best done when the sun or moon is in Aries, Leo, or Sagittarius, on Sunday, Tuesday, or Thursday, and during the hours that correspond to Mars or the sun (see Chapter 9). The Spring Equinox and the Summer Solstice are ideal times to work fire magick.

Fire magick may involve physical fire, such as the fertility fires at Beltane rites, or the element's spiritual, symbolic qualities—or both. Because fire is associated with creativity, artists can benefit from using fire magick to enhance their talents or to promote themselves and their work. Its stimulating properties can be channeled to increase your vitality, to help you overcome obstacles, to bolster self-confidence and courage, or to heighten sexual passion. Fire is also associated with purification, so spells, rituals, and practices that involve destruction and regeneration may tap the energy of this element.

Here is a fire magick spell that burns away old, self-limiting attitudes and behaviors so you can actualize your potential more fully. You'll need a sheet of paper, a pen or pencil, a cauldron or ordinary metal saucepan, matches or a lighter, and a safe place to work with fire (such as a fireplace, wood stove, range top, or barbecue grill). Do this spell a few days before the new moon.

1. See Chapter 11 and follow instructions for casting a circle.

2. Relax, put your mind at ease, and focus all your attention on the project before you.

3. Tear the sheet of paper into strips about an inch wide and two or three inches long.

4. On each strip, write an attitude, behavior, practice, or emotion that you believe is limiting you, such as fear, resentment, or intolerance.

5. When you've written down all the things you want to eliminate, place your cauldron or pan on the wood stove, grill, range, or fireplace and hold the first strip of paper above it.

6. Light the paper strip and, as it burns, say "I am released from the harmful effects of fear (or whatever you've written on the paper). Fear no longer interferes with my happiness, success, or well-being." As you do this, imagine the inner flame of spirit is purging you of the unwanted emotion.

7. Drop the strip of paper into the cauldron or pan before the flame reaches your fingers and allow it to finish

burning completely. (If you prefer, you can hold the paper strips with metal tongs to prevent accidents.)

8. Light the next paper strip and repeat the process. Continue until you've burned up all your unwanted, self-limiting attitudes and emotions.

9. Open the circle and thank the deities who have assisted you in your spellworking.

10. Now employ one of the other three elements to get rid of the ashes—scatter them in the wind (air), bury them in the ground (earth), dump them in a body of water or flush them down the toilet (water).

Earth

The ground beneath us, which provides us with a stable foundation and nourishment, is an apt symbol for the earth element. We connect this element with security, permanence, structure, the physical body, and the material realm. Earth is the element of form; it embodies spirit and makes it manifest.

Earth is one of the two elements that symbolize the feminine or yin principle. Taurus, Virgo, and Capricorn are the three earth signs of the zodiac. In tarot, the suit of disks or pentacles (shown as coins in some decks) represents the earth element. Brown, gray, tan, and green are "earth" colors. The square and the numbers four and eight are also associated with the earth element.

We see earth energy functioning in processes that involve planning and gradual development—the growth of plants, the construction of buildings, the day-to-day operation of a business or financial endeavor. People whose birthcharts feature many planets in earth signs tend to be practical, sensual, stubborn, traditional, cautious, dependable, and methodical.

Earth Magick

Earth magick is most successful if performed while the sun or moon is in Taurus, Virgo, or Capricorn, on Friday or Saturday, and during the hours that correspond to Venus or Saturn (see Chapter 9). Beltane is an ideal time to work earth magick.

Earth magick may involve physical matter (for example, soil, salt, stones) or the element's spiritual, symbolic qualities, or both. Because we connect the earth element with money and material goods, prosperity spells often harness earth energy. Do the spell below during times that relate to Taurus and Venus and when the moon is waxing. You'll need a large glass jar or ceramic bowl and some pennies.

1. Relax, put your mind at ease, and focus all your attention on the project before you. If you wish, cast a circle according to the directions in Chapter 11 or envision yourself surrounded by protective white light.

2. Drop the pennies one at a time into the jar or bowl. Each time you put in a penny, say or think, "This coin is now multiplied one hundredfold, in harmony with Divine Will and for the good of all concerned. Thank you."

3. Add at least one penny every day, repeating the affirmation with each penny you add.

4. If you are familiar with feng shui, place the jar or bowl in the wealth/prosperity gua of your home.

5. When the jar or bowl is filled, take the pennies to the bank and begin again.

Air

The air element encompasses the mental plane, ideas, language, and abstract thought. Arroyo interprets air as "the world of archetypal ideas behind the veil of the physical world." Like the wind, which is an appropriate symbol for this element, air is changeable and without form, restless and impossible to contain.

A masculine or yang force, air is an outer-directed and active element. The zodiac signs Gemini, Libra, and Aquarius comprise this element in astrology. In the tarot, the air element is represented by the suit of swords. Its numbers are five and 11, its colors are yellow and blue. A distinctly "human" energy, the air element is present in most of our interpersonal exchanges. Just as the wind physically picks up seeds from one place and carries them to another where they take root and grow, so do ideas spread and germinate among people via language. Individuals with an abundance of air energy in their birthcharts are mentally oriented, sociable, inquisitive, detached, changeable, inventive, and often impractical.

Air Magick

We employ the air element in virtually all magickal work, for it signifies the power of thought and the ability to use imagination. Incantations and affirmations, which play a role in most spells and rituals, also make use of this elemental energy.

You can use air magick to improve human relations, to enhance mental or creative abilities, as an aid while traveling, and to facilitate communication in business, legal, or personal situations. Air magick is best performed while the sun or moon is in Gemini, Libra, or Aquarius, on Wednesday or Friday, and during the hours that correspond to Mercury and Venus (see Chapter 9). Imbolc and the Fall Equinox are good times to work air magick.

The spell below can help bridge the gap between you and someone with whom you've become estranged. If you've lost touch with a person or cannot reach him/her through ordinary channels, this spell restores communication between you. If you've harmed someone, use this spell to apologize and make amends on the spirit plane when you cannot do so in another manner.

1. Relax, put your mind at ease, close your eyes, and focus all your attention on the project before you.

2. Call the person by name and ask him/her to listen to what you have to say. (If you sense this isn't a convenient time for the other person, ask when you can try again.)

3. Imagine the person you wish to communicate with is standing at the end of a road and you are at the beginning of the same road. Envision yourself traveling along the road toward this person, taking time to observe the entire journey in as much detail as possible.

4. As you journey toward this person, you'll notice a number of obstacles—stones, fallen branches, flooded areas— in the road. These obstacles represent the problems or situations that are separating you.

5. Whenever you come to an obstacle, visualize a strong, healing wind blowing it out of the way so that you can continue on your way. If your purpose is to apologize to someone you've harmed, say you're sorry each time the wind blows an obstacle from your path.

6. When all the obstacles between you have been blown away, you arrive at your destination and stand face-to-face with the individual with whom you want to communicate.

7. Say whatever you want to say to this person. Notice his/ her reaction. Thank the person for listening.

8. Open your eyes and know that your message has been heard.

Incense, which combines the properties of air and fire, can also be used to convey messages or prayers to beings in the spirit realm. Light the incense, then direct your message or prayer to whomever you wish to reach and envision your words drifting upward in the incense smoke. If you are trying to communicate with a human being rather than a deity, the incense will carry your intention to that person's higher self.

Water

Emotions, intuition, dreams, mystery, instincts, and imagination belong to the water element. Like its physical counterpart, water is fluid and ever-changing. And like the sea, its energy can be calm or turbulent—it may buoy us along or engulf us. Water is the force that connects us with other people and which allows us to respond to stimuli in our environment. Liz Greene says, "The element of water, astrologically, is the most enigmatic of all the elements...furthest from the rational realm."

Water is one of the two elements that symbolize the feminine, or yin, principle. The astrological signs Cancer, Scorpio, and Pisces comprise the water element; in the tarot, the suit of cups equates with water. In feng shui, things that are cool, damp, dark, or yielding belong to the water element. Deep blue, sea green, and violet are water colors. People whose birthcharts contain an abundance of water energy are sensitive, impressionable, intuitive, reclusive, changeable, imaginative, and impractical.

Water Magick

Because we connect intuition and feeling with water, this element is present in most magickal work. Sometimes water magick involves actual water or other liquids. For example, baptism is a form of water magick (although many Christians might take issue with this). Scrying, channeling, past-life regression, and divination are magickal practices that utilize the water element.

Emotions and relationships partake of the water element, so water magick can be effective in love spells. Water magick can be beneficial to artists, musicians, healers, and people who want to enhance their creative or intuitive abilities. Water is also associated with cleansing, therefore it is often used for purification practices. It's best to perform water magick while the sun or moon is in Cancer, Scorpio, or Pisces, on Monday, and during the hours that correspond to the moon, Neptune, or Pluto (see Chapter 9). Samhain is a good time to do water magick, especially work that involves divination or using your intuition.

Scrying (seeing images with your inner sight) is a common form of water magick, described in many myths and fairytales. It can be done with any smooth, polished surface. Some people like to gaze into the depths of a crystal ball, others prefer to use a sheet of black glass or a pool of water. As with any other art, some people are naturally more gifted at scrying than others and it may take you awhile to become proficient—don't get discouraged if you don't achieve results immediately.

1. Relax and put your mind at ease. Breathe slowly and deeply, focusing on your breath.

2. If you wish, cast a circle according to the directions in Chapter 11 or envision yourself surrounded by protective white light.

3. When you are ready, gaze into your scrying surface. Don't try to focus too closely, just let your eyes rest on the scrying tool.

4. If you are seeking an answer to a specific question, ask it now. Otherwise, just open yourself to whatever visions come.

5. Allow your mind to drift. Remain present in the moment, but try not to think about anything specific. The mental state is usually similar to what's achieved during meditation—calm receptivity—although some people experience a deeper trance.

6. Wait for visions to appear before your eyes. Don't try to force them, let them come on their own. When they do, observe them as if you were watching a movie—pay attention without directing the action.

7. Also notice any emotions or impressions you sense as you observe the visions.

8. Let the scenario play out in its entirety. Trust that what you see is accurate and has meaning for you, even if you don't understand everything completely at the time.

9. Bring yourself back to ordinary consciousness and write down what you've seen and felt in as much detail as possible.

Chapter 5

The Astrological Year

"Astrology...[shows us]...that there is a rhythm to the universe and that man's own life partakes of this rhythm."

—Henry Miller

In early cultures, the new year began on the Spring Equinox—the day the sun enters Aries, the first sign of the zodiac—rather than on January 1. The sun's movement though the heavens, against a backdrop of constellations, provided logical divisions for the wheel of the year. In the tropical zodiac, the sun's physical position no longer coincides with its astrological position. (See "precession of the equinoxes" in the glossary.)

Undoubtedly, you are familiar with your sun sign—the astrological sign in which the sun was positioned at the time of your birth—and how this influences your personality. But the sun's passage through the 12 zodiacal signs can also be seen as a cycle that describes the evolution of consciousness, a symbolic journey of inception, growth, assimilation, actualization, dissolution, death, and rebirth.

Aries

Each year the sun enters Aries on the Spring Equinox, around March 20, and remains there through approximately April 19 (this can vary slightly from year to year). This is the period of inception, the starting point, the beginning of new life, when the earth awakens with a burst of enthusiasm from her long winter's sleep. Aries' energy is raw, primal, vigorous, dynamic, assertive, spontaneous, masculine. A cardinal fire sign, Aries represents spirit in action, inspiration, and the drive to break free from the collective and express the self as an independent entity.

For personal growth

This is the time to assert yourself, to push for what you want. While the sun is in Aries, connect with nature's first rush of vitality and move outward into the world, embracing life's challenges. Focus on yourself and what you need to be fulfilled. Be daring, take chances, meet new people, initiate projects, experiment, have fun. Don't deliberate, act.

In magickal work

While the sun is in Aries, perform magick to inspire, bless, or activate new endeavors, especially those that you want to come to fruition within a short period of time. This is a good month to work magick to overcome obstacles, meet challenges, break away from another person's influence, or stimulate movement in stagnant or blocked situations. Spells to increase physical vitality can also benefit from the energy of Aries.

Taurus

The sun is in Taurus from approximately April 20 until May 20. This is a period of fertilization and growth, when the earth begins to blossom. Seeds planted during Aries now germinate and start to grow. Ideas conceived during the previous sign are developed and take shape in the material world. Taurus' energy is slow and steady, nurturing, stabilizing, tactile, enduring, fruitful, acquisitive, feminine. A fixed earth sign, Taurus represents manifestation, the urge to form a creative union through which something tangible and permanent can be built.

For personal growth

This is the time to bring ideas down to earth and apply them in practical ways. Use your resources—talents, money, and physical abilities—to produce something functional and lasting. Financial and material considerations may become a focus now. While the sun is in Taurus, examine your values and what enhances your self-worth. Pay attention to beauty, experience the sensory realm, enjoy your body, establish bonds with other people, be creative.

In magickal work

While the sun is in Taurus, do magick to generate abundance of all kinds. This is a good month to work spells for prosperity, career success, love, fertility, artistic inspiration, and security. Sex magick can be very effective now. Taurus' energy can also help increase physical strength or sexual prowess.

Gemini

The sun is in Gemini from approximately May 20 through June 20. This is a period of interaction and dispersion. Energy that solidified during Taurus is now liberated and moves about freely from place to place. As you expand outwardly from a small circle of loved ones to the larger community, social activities and exchanging information become important. Gemini's energy is mental, changeable, curious, adaptable, versatile, quick, androgynous. A mutable air sign, Gemini represents the impulse to learn, experience, and share with others.

For personal growth

This is the time to expand your network of personal contacts, to develop friendships and business associations, to get involved in your community. Explore the world of ideas and communicate with other people. Learn new skills, read, write, study, stretch your mental capabilities, indulge your curiosity.

In magickal work

While the sun is in Gemini, focus on using mental imagery and affirmations in your magickal work. Study magickal traditions and practices, or become affiliated with a group of like-minded individuals. This is a good time to connect with your spirit guides, use telepathy to contact people you can't reach through ordinary channels, or send messages or requests to deities. Spells to facilitate business transactions or communication with other people can benefit from Gemini's energy.

Cancer

The sun enters Cancer on the Summer Solstice, around June 21, and remains in this sign through approximately July 21. Cancer represents the urge to put down roots, to connect with your heritage and your past, to establish secure foundations in the human community, and to protect all that is near and dear to you. Energy that was scattered freely while the sun was in Gemini is now gathered in and devoted to nurturing the inner self. A cardinal water sign, Cancer is sensitive, private, emotional, nurturing, unstable, possessive, feminine.

For personal growth

This is the time to turn inward and nurture your sense of personal power, security, and emotional stability. You may wish to examine your childhood and how experiences in your youth are still influencing you now. Family relationships can also be strengthened or explored during this period.

In magickal work

While the sun is in Cancer, work on developing your intuition. This is also a good time to perform fertility magick, to bless and protect home and/or family members, or to do past-life regression work.

Leo

The sun is in Leo from approximately July 22 through August 22. This is the period of fertility and reproduction, when crops are ripe and the earth is rich with abundance. Now is the time to indulge your creativity in myriad ways. Focus your attention on the things you love, that give you a sense of fulfillment, purpose, and identity—these are your gifts to the world. Leo's energy is exuberant, radiant, magnanimous, self-centered, dramatic, masculine. A fixed fire sign, Leo represents the urge to express yourself and to produce offspring, whether these are children of the mind or of the body.

For personal growth

This is the time to express yourself in a creative manner, whether or not you think of yourself as an artist. Discover what's special about you and apply your talents in ways that give you pleasure. Let your personal beauty shine. Relax, enjoy yourself, have fun, socialize, be affectionate. Focus on yourself and what makes you happy.

In magickal work

While the sun is in Leo, do magick to improve your self-esteem, leadership ability, status, career position, or public image. Creative people can benefit from practices that enhance imagination and productivity. Love spells can also be very effective now.

Virgo

The sun is in Virgo from approximately August 22 through September 22. This is the harvest period, when you reap what was sown in the spring. Often a busy time of the year, this month equates with work. Virgo represents the impulse to do something useful in the world and to be of service to others. A mutable earth sign, Virgo is orderly, practical, compassionate, modest, analytical, sensitive, feminine.

For personal growth

This is the time to devote yourself to work and work relationships. Bring ideas down to earth and find useful ways to apply them. Be efficient, refine procedures, get organized, tie up loose ends. Clean up your diet and take care of your health now, too.

In magickal work

Spells and rituals to improve your job situation and/or interactions with coworkers and colleagues can be effective while the sun is in Virgo. This is also a good time to do healing work and to utilize the magickal properties of plants. Pay attention to the earth and its bounty and to animal totems who can assist you.

Libra

The sun enters Libra on the Autumn Equinox, around September 22, and remains in this sign through approximately October 22. This is a period of unification and partnership. Libra represents the urge to complement your own energies with those of another person, to balance yin and yang in a harmonious manner. During this phase in the cycle of growth, individual desires are less important than the relationship. A cardinal air sign, Libra is adaptable, refined, passive, calm, indecisive, unemotional, objective.

For personal growth

This is the time to work on strengthening partnerships in love and/or business. Learn to compromise and respect the needs of others as well as your own. Seek fairness and balance in all relationships. Rather than pursuing personal goals, focus on helping others with theirs for the good of all.

In magickal work

Love spells are most successful when performed while the sun is in Libra. This is also a good time to do magick to improve work relationships or to attract people who can help you further your social and/or professional objectives.

Scorpio

The sun is in Scorpio from approximately October 23 through November 21. This is the period of death and re-birth, when the remains of the harvest are plowed under to decay and fertilize the earth. At this time, the life force withdraws from the world of activity and turns inward. Scorpio's energy is passionate, subterranean, intense, destructive, regenerative, controlling, feminine. A fixed water sign, Scorpio represents the urge to plumb the depths of emotional experience and to destroy old structures in order to make room for something new to emerge.

For personal growth

This is the time to eliminate old habits and behaviors that have been holding you back. Issues involving control and/or power may arise now. Examine long-standing fears, blocks, and emotional patterns/conditions stemming from childhood or past lifetimes. Psychological counseling can be helpful during this period.

In magickal work

Scorpio is associated with magick, occult power, and the hidden realms, so this is a good time to do most types of magickal work. Shapeshifting, past-life regression, sex magick, divination, journeying, and prosperity spells in particular, can benefit from Scorpio's energy.

Sagittarius

The sun is in Sagittarius from approximately November 22 through December 20. This is a period of growth and expansion, which usually involves some kind of questing. Knowledge and experience of all sorts are sought in order to enrich life at every level. Sagittarius' energy is restless, curious, sociable, lively, changeable, optimistic, boundless, masculine. A mutable fire sign, Sagittarius represents the urge to push beyond present limits, to pursue dreams and ideals, and to share discoveries with other people.

For personal growth

This is the time to seek knowledge of all kinds. Spiritual studies, mythology, psychology, and philosophy can provide valuable insights now. During this period you may also benefit from traveling and learning about other cultures in order to increase your understanding of the world and your place in it.

In magickal work

Expand your knowledge of magickal traditions through study and practice while the sun is in Sagittarius. This is also a good time to go on a vision quest or do journeying work. Dance and music might also provide insights and awakenings now.

Capricorn

The sun enters Capricorn on the Winter Solstice, around December 21, and remains in this sign through approximately January 19. The sun has passed its lowest point and the days are growing longer. This is a period of achievement in the outer world, of recognizing and performing your role in life's drama. Capricorn's energy is practical, enduring, tenacious, steady, materialistic, reserved, feminine. A cardinal earth sign, Capricorn represents the urge to accomplish goals, create stability and structure, and build for the future.

For personal growth

This is the time to concentrate on career objectives and/or making your mark in the world. Lay foundations for the future, set goals, establish yourself in your community, and pursue plans in a steady, organized fashion. Focus on practical matters and on bringing your dreams to fruition.

In magickal work

While the sun is in Capricorn, perform magick to get a job, advance in your profession, or improve your public image. This is a good time to do prosperity spells or to bless a business.

Aquarius

The sun is in Aquarius from approximately January 20 through February 18. This is a period of breaking down old structures and ushering in new ideas. Rigid hierarchies are replaced with more egalitarian situations that benefit humanity in general rather than a privileged few. Aquarius' energy is rebellious, independent, friendly, impersonal, unpredictable, idealistic, masculine. A fixed air sign, Aquarius represents the urge for change and freedom.

For personal growth

This is the time to make changes in your life. Open yourself up to new experiences and people. Don't be afraid to take a few risks. Be spontaneous. Enjoy friendships, group activities, and intellectual pursuits. Express what's unique about you and don't worry about what others may think.

In magickal work

Aquarius is the sign of astrology and this is a good time to study or utilize astrological knowledge. Do magick that promotes change, breaks up stagnant conditions, or stimulates action. Working with a group could be advantageous now.

Pisces

The sun is in Pisces from approximately February 18 through March 20. This is a period of dissolution, of transcending physical boundaries in order to connect with the collective unconscious and the Divine. Inspiration may come from higher realms, enhancing imagination and creativity. Pisces' energy is gentle, compassionate, artistic, emotional, secretive, idealistic, feminine. A mutable water sign, Pisces represents the desire for complete merger, to sacrifice the individual self for a higher good.

For personal growth

This is the time to examine your dreams for insights and guidance. Meditation or periods of withdrawal from the outer world can help you get in touch with yourself at a deep level. Listen to music. Paint. Write poetry. Rather than striving for perfection, give your imagination free rein; suspend judgment, and enjoy the process.

In magickal work

While the sun is in Pisces, you may find that your connection with the spiritual realms is strengthened; communication with angelic guides, ancestors, or other people's higher selves becomes easier now. Your psychic abilities are enhanced by Pisces' energy—trust your intuition. You may also experience increased healing powers. This is a particularly good time to do dreamwork and divination.

Chapter 6

The Wheel of the Year

"Nothing exists nor happens in the visible sky that is not sensed in some hidden moment by the faculties of Earth and Nature."
—Johannes Kepler

Many of the holidays we mark today have their roots in the ancient Pagan festivals, or Sabbats, which were based on solar cycles. Still celebrated by neo-Pagans today, these eight Sabbats chart the sun's annual passage through the heavens beginning on the Winter Solstice, the shortest day of the year, when the Sun King is reborn from the depths of winter's darkness. Subsequent holidays follow at intervals of approximately six weeks and tell the story of the king's growth, maturity, decline, death, and rebirth.

The quarter days divide the wheel of the year at the Solstices and Equinoxes. These dates mark the sun's ingress into the four cardinal signs of the zodiac—the Spring Equinox occurs at 0 degrees Aries, the Summer Solstice at 0 degrees Cancer, the Fall Equinox at 0 degrees Libra, and the Winter Solstice at 0 degrees Capricorn.

The cross quarter days—Imbolc (im´ bolk), Beltane (bel´ taine), Lughnasadh (loo´ na saad), and Samhain (sow´ en)—divide the periods between the quarter days in half. Some Pagans celebrate these holidays on the days when the sun reaches 15 degrees of the fixed signs: Taurus, Leo, Scorpio, and Aquarius. Others mark the sabbats on the 31st to the 2nd of the corresponding solar months.

As Starhawk writes in *The Spiral Dance*, "The Sabbats are the eight points at which we connect the inner and the outer cycles; the interstices where the seasonal, the celestial, the communal, the creative, and the personal all meet."

Winter Solstice or Yule

Long before the advent of Christianity, earth-centered cultures in Europe, Britain, and Ireland commemorated the birth of the Sun King at the Winter Solstice, which falls around December 21, varying slightly from year to year. This is the longest night of the year (in the Northern Hemisphere), after which daylight is on the ascent and darkness begins to recede. A joyous time, heralding promise and renewal, Yule celebrates the triumph of the forces of light over darkness, of life over death. The holiday was so important to Pagan cultures that Christianity adopted this season of good cheer to mark the birth of Jesus.

Celebrating Yule

The Christmas tree has its origins in the Pagan winter festivals of northern Europe and the British Isles. Because evergreens retain their foliage even during the coldest months, when other plants die or lose their leaves, they symbolize everlasting life. Therefore, they play a central role in Yule festivities (as they do during the Christmas season). In recognition of the rebirth of life when the earth appears dead and barren, neo-Pagans decorate their homes with pine, holly, cedar, and other evergreens.

In a magickal sense, pine's cleansing properties can help eliminate negative energies. Holly was sacred to the Druids. According to Celtic mythology, holly bushes provided shelter for the nature spirits during the winter. The Druids also valued mistletoe as an herb of fertility and immortality. Used in talismans as an aphrodisiac (perhaps the reason we kiss beneath it today), mistletoe is said to enhance creativity of all kinds. Its magickal properties offer protection, which is where we get the holiday custom of hanging it on doorways and in entrance halls of our homes. Circular evergreen wreaths symbolize eternity, wholeness, and unity.

The Yule log (traditionally oak) is lit on the eve of the Winter Solstice and allowed to burn throughout the night. (Save a piece of unburned wood to include in next year's fire.) You may wish to include wood from other sacred trees— hazel, alder, rowan, hawthorn, birch, willow, holly, apple, yew, and ash—in your holiday fire. After the fire burns down, collect ashes and wrap them in a piece of silk or linen with a pinecone. Then place the package under your pillow at night to solicit guidance and advice from your guardian angel.

Greenery, bark, roots, and so on from these trees can also be brewed in a cauldron over the ritual fire. Drain the fragrant brew, allow the mixture to dry, then fashion sachets from the sacred blend to provide protection, health, and blessings throughout the year.

Feasting, music, exchanging gifts, dancing, and singing are part of many Yule festivities, as they are at Christmas. Some people enact a play of the Sun King's birth. You may wish to design your own ritual to commemorate the occasion and personalize it in a way that has meaning for you. (Starhawk's *Spiral Dance*, Morwyn's *Secrets of a Witch's Coven*, and Lira Silbury's *Sacred Marriage* offer suggestions, as do many other books on neo-Pagan and Wiccan traditions.)

Imbolc, Candlemas, or Brigid's Day

Celebrated between February 1 and 5 (depending on the sun's position and your preference), when the sun is in Aquarius, Imbolc honors the Celtic goddess Brigid. When

Christianity became widespread in Ireland and the British Isles, Brigid was named a saint because the Celtic Pagans refused to abandon their beloved goddess. Also known as the Lady of the Flame or Bright One, she is the goddess of poetry, healing, and smithcraft. Creativity is her gift to humanity, symbolized by the fire of inspiration which she tends. Imbolc means "in the belly" and the cauldron, representing the womb where creativity is nurtured, is one of her tools.

At this stage in the wheel of the year, the young Sun King is beginning to grow. Daylight is increasing (in the Northern Hemisphere), winter is on the wane, and spring's renewal is promised. Thus, Brigid's Day is a reaffirmation of life and a time for planting "seeds," in the form of ideas and affirmations, that you want to ripen as the year matures.

Celebrating Imbolc

Fire is the central feature at Imbolc, and you may choose to light a sacred fire as part of your ritual. If you are celebrating the holiday with others, give each person a candle. Form a circle around a ritual fire or a large pillar candle set on an altar in the center of the circle. Also place a cauldron filled with sand or earth on the altar.

One by one, each person lights his or her candle from the central flame. When all are lit, one person begins by stating a "seed" wish for the coming year (in the form of an affirmation). Go around the circle, letting everyone affirm for what he or she wants the year to bring. As smoke from the candles rises toward the heavens, it carries your requests to Brigid. Songs or prayers of thanks may also be offered at this time. When you are ready to break up the circle, place the candles upright in the cauldron and allow them to burn down completely.

Because Brigid is the goddess of inspiration and creativity, you honor her by firing your imagination. I always spend her day engaged in some form of artistic activity, usually writing and painting. Some friends of mine bake, others fashion wreaths of greenery and pinecones. If you have smithing skills or healing powers, this is the perfect opportunity to use them.

Spring Equinox or Ostara

The sun's ingress into Aries around March 20 marks the Spring Equinox. Today, the hours of daylight and night are equal in length. Flowers are starting to bloom, trees begin to bud with new leaves, and in some parts of the Northern Hemisphere, it's warm enough to begin planting crops. In the Sun King's journey, this is a period of growth and power, the point at which light surpasses darkness.

Celebrating the Spring Equinox

The Equinoxes are times of balance, when daylight—which corresponds to activity, the outer world, and masculine energy—is equal to night—rest, the inner world, and feminine energy. On this day, devote an equal amount of time to both. For example, I try to complement periods of physical activity with meditation, socializing with solitude, work with rest. Practices that combine male and female energies are also appropriate for this holiday.

Because Ostara is the first day of spring, it is a good time to plant seeds (literally or figuratively) and to gather, plant, or decorate your home with flowers. A friend of mine makes flower garlands for herself and her children to wear on this day. Magick that utilizes flowers, herbs, and other botanicals can be especially powerful if performed on the Spring Equinox. The Druids celebrated the Festival of Trees on this day. In honor of my Druid ancestors, I hang offerings—talismans, fetishes, crystals, ribbons, and other tokens—from the branches of trees on Ostara. Ideally, you'll want to perform Spring Equinox festivities outdoors.

Like all of the Sabbats that take place while the sun is waxing, Ostara is a fertility holiday. Painting eggs, which symbolize new life and promise, is a traditional way to commemorate this aspect of the Spring Equinox. This is the origin of the custom of decorating eggs at Easter (a word that derives from Ostara or Eostar).

With the arrival of spring, we say goodbye to the winter season of scarcity and hardship. The Equinox is also a time for leaving behind old fears and self-limiting attitudes or behaviors as you look ahead with hope to a brighter future. You can act this out symbolically by wrapping a cord several times around your wrists to represent psychological bonds that are holding you back. Chant a phrase that describes what you want to change in your life, such as "I release neediness and embrace success." As you envision this taking place, wriggle your hands until your bonds loosen and come undone.

Beltane

Beltane is celebrated on May 1 or on May 5-6 when the sun reaches 15 degrees of Taurus. This joyful time of the year honors nature, creativity, and fertility, which are associated with earthy Taurus. The word comes from the old name for the sun god, Baal or Bel. Beltane recognizes the time of the year when crops are planted and flowers bloom. The Sun King has now reached maturity and is ready to take a mate: the earth.

Celebrating Beltane

Because Beltane is connected with fertility, it celebrates sexuality, and the Great Rite is often a part of the holiday's festivities. In pre-Christian Europe, sexual rites were considered a type of sympathetic magick performed to enhance the earth's fertility. The Maypole is an obvious phallic symbol; dancing around it recognizes the union of male and female energies for the purpose of creativity—of the mind as well as the body. In some early cultures, women who wished to become pregnant leapt over small fires on Beltane and domestic animals were led between fires to increase their fertility.

Beltane is a joyful holiday and may be greeted with dancing, singing, drumming, or other forms of cheerful celebration. Activities that honor creativity, especially in connection with love, are also appropriate on this day. Each year on this Sabbat, a group of friends and I publish a book of erotic poems and stories.

This is also a time to commune with the nature spirits and to honor the earth. Beltane rites may include making offerings to the earth and nature deities, feasting on the earth's bounty, and planting seeds that will produce new life. If possible, celebrate this holiday outdoors.

Summer Solstice or Midsummer

The sun's ingress into Cancer on approximately June 21 marks the Summer Solstice, the longest day of the year. The Sun King has now reached the peak of his powers and reigns at the summit of the heavens.

Celebrating the Summer Solstice

This is a time of fullness, to enjoy feasting and revelry and the richness of life. Ideally, this holiday should be celebrated outdoors. This is a good day to gather herbs and other natural materials to use in spells and talismans. Decorate your home with flowers. The Summer Solstice is also a time to give thanks for nature's bounty and for personal successes. "Seeds" that were sown earlier in the year now bear fruit. Remember the nature spirits and earth elementals at this time of the year and leave offerings for them.

The sun's position high in the sky chases away shadows and darkness, enhancing clarity and vision. Therefore, some people choose to practice divination or embark on vision quests today. However, the fullness of the sun's power is best utilized in an active, social, outward manner. Celebrate with music and dancing. Play, laugh, have fun. Put aside solemnity and introspection temporarily while you share this holiday with friends, loved ones, and people of like mind.

Lughnasadh or Lammas

Named for the Celtic god Lugh, Lughnasadh is celebrated on August 1, or around August 7 when the sun reaches 15 degrees of Leo. This is the first of the waning festivals, when the sun's light is declining and we begin to harvest the season's crops. The Sun King's powers begin to ebb as he ages, although his mate—the earth—reaches a period of abundance now.

Celebrating Lughnasadh

Because Lughnasadh coincides with the season when grains are ripe in many parts of the northern hemisphere, baking bread is usually part of this holiday celebration. Beer and ale, which are made from grain, also play a role in Lughnasadh festivities and many people enjoy brewing their own grain-based beverages on this day. You may also wish to decorate your home with sheaves of grain, berries, and late summer flowers.

In some traditions, a facsimile of the Sun King is fashioned from grain. Stalks of grain can be woven together to form a doll or a loaf of bread may be baked in the shape of a man. Build a ritual fire (outdoors if possible) and give thanks to the earth and the sun whose combined energies produced the grain. Then toss the grain man into the fire to symbolize the death of the Sun King as the year wanes.

Like many of the Pagan holidays, Lughnasadh honors nature, so remember to give thanks for her bounty today. If possible, spend some time outdoors. I usually take a long walk in the woods or in the park near my home to commune with the nature spirits. I also leave offerings of bread for the earth elementals.

Autumn Equinox or Mabon

The Fall Equinox occurs on approximately September 22, when the sun enters Libra. Traditionally, this coincides with the harvest season and is therefore a time to give thanks for the bounty in our lives. The season of fullness and activity is over, a period of rest and introspection is approaching. Because the day and night are the same length today, this is also a time of balance.

Celebrating the Autumn Equinox

Focus on the ebb and flow in your own life today. Seek balance between your inner and outer worlds, between yourself and others, between action and contemplation, work and relaxation. You may wish to offer thanks for all you've received during the past six months—physically, mentally, spiritually, emotionally. Making an offering to the gods and goddesses is also appropriate now.

As you reflect upon your past and what you want the future to bring, weave a braid of natural material (hemp, linen cloth, straw, silk cord, and the like) which represents those things you plan to weave into your life. The three strands symbolize body, mind, and spirit. Concentrate on your wishes as you braid your magickal cord. This is a link between you and the Divine, serving as a conduit through which assistance comes from the spiritual world. When you've finished, hang the cord someplace where you'll see it often. Throughout the dark season ahead, work in harmony with Divine Will to achieve your wishes.

You may want to decorate your home with pinecones, nuts, fall leaves, dried cornstalks, or dried flowers on Mabon. Some people build a ritual fire and burn these in it to honor the dying Sun King. This is also a good time to make wine from the season's harvest and to share a holiday meal of fall vegetables with loved ones.

Samhain or Halloween

Also known as All Hallows' Eve and Hallowmass, Samhain is usually celebrated on October 31, although some people mark the holiday on November 7 - 8, when the sun reaches 15 degrees of Scorpio. Long nights and cold weather descend upon the earth as the Sun King's powers decline. This is the season of death and rebirth, when the dregs of the harvest are plowed under to decay and fertilize the earth. In Wiccan and neo-Pagan traditions, it is a solemn time for remembering and honoring those who have passed into the other realm.

Celebrating Samhain

The final Sabbat in the wheel of the year, Samhain is the time for reflecting on the past and looking ahead to the future. Both an ending and a beginning, it is a day for releasing old ideas, outworn behaviors, unwanted habits, and restrictive bonds in order to make room for something new to be born. Some people write down on strips of paper all the things they want to eliminate from their lives—fears, self-limiting attitudes, unhealthy attachments—and burn them in a ritual fire on Samhain Eve.

Because Samhain is the Witches' new year, it is also an appropriate time to make new year's wishes or resolutions. Originally, the custom of wearing costumes on Halloween was a way to visually demonstrate what you wanted to be in the coming year and to project that image out into the world. (No witch would choose to dress up as a ghost, skeleton, goblin, or hobo!)

On Samhain, the veil between the worlds is thinner than at any other time of the year, making it easier to communicate with spirit guides, nonphysical entities, and departed loved ones. Consequently, this is a good time for scrying and divination. Dreams on Samhain may have special significance, too.

You may wish to decorate your home with apples, pumpkins, acorns, and other fruits of the harvest season. Ritual fires made from the wood of the sacred trees are also a traditional part of the Samhain celebration. Some groups enact dramas that portray the death of the old year and the birth of the new, or the passage of the soul from one realm to another.

Chapter 7

Astrology and the Natural World

"The theory of correspondences is the rationale behind the esoteric teaching that the position of the stars will influence thought, mood, perception, and gestalt."

—James Wasserman

Everything in our physical world corresponds to one of the bodies in the heavenly realm. These correspondences are based on energetic similarities between earthly matters and celestial influences. You're already familiar with birthstones—gems related to the signs of the zodiac—but you probably didn't realize that this concept of affinities includes virtually everything on our planet.

In astrological parlance, the sun, moon, and planets are said to rule, or have dominion over, living things, inanimate objects, and activities—just about every facet of our existence, in fact. At one time, the heavenly bodies were considered to be the embodiments of deities who presided over affairs on earth, and each god or goddess had certain responsibilities, hence the concept of rulership. You don't have to subscribe to this belief to work magick; however, it is important to know which things are linked with which planet or sign. Utilizing the inherent energies of various substances, such as herbs, metals, gemstones, and colors, can enhance the power of a spell.

In Chapter 4, you learned about the basic natures and characteristics of the sun, moon, and planets, as well as the four elements. As you work with these energies and develop a feel for them, you'll start to understand why alcohol, for instance, is associated with Neptune, and why computers are related to Uranus. In this chapter, I provide numerous lists that show the correspondences between zodiac signs and many objects you might wish to incorporate in your magickal work. You'll find a much more comprehensive body of information in Rex E. Bills' *The Rulership Book*.

When working spells, consider the nature or purpose of your spell and the astrological sign associated with that purpose. Love spells, for example, correspond to Libra, the sign of relationships, and Venus, the planet that rules Libra. Then choose substances that have an affinity with the appropriate sign or heavenly body.

In some cases, you may wish to work with objects that relate to astrological factors in your own birthchart or the chart of the person for whom you are doing the spell. Gemstones, herbs, metals, colors, and other natural materials can help strengthen weak factors in an individual's natal chart. For example, an "idea" person who has a preponderance of air signs in his or her birthchart and wants to be able to apply those ideas in practical ways could wear stones or scents that are connected with the earth signs Taurus, Virgo, or Capricorn. Healing spells might incorporate specially chosen stones, botanicals, and so on to energize debilitated factors in an ailing person's chart or to modify the difficult influences of transiting planets.

Magickal Gems

For centuries, gemstones have been worn to attract luck, health, love, and prosperity. Until recently, gemstones were prized for their magickal properties, not their monetary ones.

Magickal practitioners still utilize stones and crystals in their work to augment the power of magickal tools, to attract and focus healing energies, or as ingredients in spells and talismans.

A birthstone is a gem whose vibration harmonizes with a person's sun sign. Some psychics and sensitive individuals can actually see or feel the vibrations that emanate from stones, just as they might see or sense a person's aura. Because stones are so dense and inherently durable, they hold vibrations for a very long time and are useful as power objects.

Gemstones can also attract certain energies for specific purposes. Early astrologers believed diamonds enhanced marital relations, which may be why modern couples still choose them for engagement rings. Many gems are believed to have protective and/or healing properties. Amber is reputed to shield the wearer from all types of danger; legend says it can also keep you from going deaf or losing your teeth. Jade is worn in the East to ensure good health. According to folklore, it protects against evil and accidents. The ancient Greeks thought jade warded off stomach and kidney problems. Amethysts are believed to calm nervous tension and bring the wearer peace of mind. Legend has it that amethyst, a favorite stone of Bacchus, will also keep you from getting drunk.

Because each astrological sign straddles two months, it's best to choose gemstones according to the sign rather than the month of birth.

Aries:	Diamond, bloodstone.
Taurus:	Emerald, star sapphire, turquoise.
Gemini:	Aquamarine, quartz, agate.
Cancer:	Pearl, moonstone.
Leo:	Ruby, amber, tiger eye.

Virgo:	Sapphire, jade, peridot, pink jasper.
Libra:	Opal, coral, lapis lazuli.
Scorpio:	Topaz, lodestone, bloodstone.
Sagittarius:	Turquoise, topaz.
Capricorn:	Onyx, jet, smoky quartz, malachite.
Aquarius:	Garnet, zircon, obsidian.
Pisces:	Amethyst, aquamarine, coral, rose quartz.

Magickal Plants

For millennia, wise men and women have used plants to cure illnesses, provide protection, attract love, induce visions, and increase prosperity. Although the physical properties of botanicals are important in healing, their mystical qualities are equally significant when you're working in the magickal realm. The etheric bodies, intelligence, and subtle energy fields of plants interact with our own and with the vibratory patterns in the cosmos to produce effects that cannot be explained in a materialistic way.

Because they are alive, plants have particularly powerful vibratory properties that you can tap in spellworking. Dried flower petals, leaves, roots, or seeds can be used in amulets and talismans. Flower extracts are a basic ingredient in many perfumes, oils, and incense.

Astrological Affinities

Hippocrates believed a physician should not attempt to treat a patient without knowing the patient's birthchart. Culpeper wrote, "First consider what planet causes the ailment...you may oppose ailments by herbs of the planet opposite to the planet that causes them."

Affinities between plants and planets are determined for a variety of reasons. Some flowers bloom during the month when the sun is in their corresponding zodiacal sign. For example, Christmas cactus usually blossoms during December. Some plants possess properties that are similar to the astrological sign with which they are associated. Hemp, for instance, is known for its hardiness, a quality astrologers connect with Capricorn. Water lilies and lotus flowers grow in water, so they are related to the water signs Cancer and Pisces.

Like gemstones, flowers are often linked with certain months; however, you should choose flowers according to birth sign, not the month of birth. The list below shows which plants are appropriate for each sign. (Note: Some plants are not edible and some may not be appropriate for use directly on the body. For more detailed information, refer to *The Master Book of Herbalism* or David Hoffmann's *New Holistic Herbal*.)

Aries:	Holly, aloe, dogwood, jonquil, hyacinth, honeysuckle, snapdragon, cactus, cayenne, basil, cumin, paprika, marjoram, dry mustard, onion, garlic.
Taurus:	Columbine, daisy, larkspur, lily, daffodil, orchid, clover, lilac, peppermint, bergamot, catnip, golden seal, lemongrass, sage, thyme, birch, ivy.
Gemini:	Azalea, honeysuckle, lily of the valley, cedar, vervain, yarrow, valerian, dill, parsley, fennel, lavender, tansy, heather, ferns, endive.
Cancer:	Iris, jasmine, water lily, white rose, anise, sesame, coriander, ginger, hyssop, lettuce, willow, watercress.

Leo: Red rose, larkspur, poppy, marigold,
                peony, dahlia, sunflower, cinnamon,
                saffron, chamomile, dill, rosemary,
                fennel, ash.

Virgo: Aster, heather, lavender, myrtle, pink
                geranium, fern, gentian, caraway, celery
                seed, sassafras, savory, valerian, aster,
                fennel, azalea, dill, mulberry.

Libra: Cosmos, apple blossom, daisy, gardenia,
                pink rose, violet, hibiscus, myrtle, sage,
                golden seal, pennyroyal, peppermint,
                thyme, wild strawberry.

Scorpio: Chrysanthemum, orchid, violet,
                dogwood, eucalyptus, foxglove,
                raspberry, hops, rye, unicorn root,
                periwinkle.

Sagittarius: Paperwhite narcissus, Christmas cactus,
                dandelion, magnolia, agrimony,
                cardamom, sandalwood, hyssop, rose
                hips, red clover, sage, maple, pinks,
                chestnut.

Capricorn: Holly, carnation, mistletoe, pansy,
                hemp, aconitum, poppy seed, carob,
                comfrey, skullcap, oak, comfrey,
                wintergreen, moss, thistle, pine.

Aquarius: Carnation, arbutus, wild rose, ginseng,
                allspice, clove, chicory, cinnamon,
                nutmeg, unicorn root, pomegranate
                seed, star anise, lady slipper.

Pisces: Violet, heather, passion flower, wisteria,
                narcissus, lotus, poppy seed, mint,
                thyme.

Creating a Magickal Garden

The garden symbolizes sanctuary, a place where we can go to escape the noise, pollution, and stress of everyday life and renew ourselves physically and spiritually. Both the Bible and the Sufi Way use the garden as an image for Paradise. In part, this restorative effect occurs because the elemental archetypes—earth, air, fire, and water—are united in the garden, producing a sense of balance and wholeness.

As you design your garden, think about how you will use it and what you hope to attain from it. Are physical and/or emotional healing priorities for you? Do you envision your garden as a place for meditation and communion with the Divine? Will you perform magickal rituals here? Will other people use your garden, too? How will it impact the rest of the environment? Also, consider the phases of the moon and other celestial cycles to find the most auspicious times to carry out your gardening plans.

You can create a magickal garden by combining the four elements, either physically or symbolically, with plants that correspond to the astrological energies you wish to emphasize in your life. Here are some suggestions:

Fire: The sun's rays provide the fire element naturally, but you might also want to hang faceted crystals (like the ones used in feng shui) or small mirrors in strategic spots to reflect sunlight and enhance this quality. At night, votive candles, lanterns, or electric lights can add a festive touch of fire to your garden.

Earth: The ground itself brings the earth element into your garden. Stones, clay pots for plants, and statuary made from ceramic or marble also embody this element.

Air: The air element is present when the wind circulates through your garden. To enhance this energy, hang a wind chime, bells, or mobile to dance and sing whenever the breeze blows. Or, combine the elements of air and fire by burning incense in your garden.

Water: Does your garden have a stream or pond? If not, a birdbath or fountain will bring the water element into your garden. If these options aren't possible, place water in a vase, shallow dish, or a hollow in a rock.

Remember that plants are complex, living entities and their presence in your garden will influence you in myriad ways, so choose species that will enhance your intentions. Choose carefully; some common plants, such as foxglove and wolfbane, are poisonous and may not be appropriate for you. I recommend consulting some good books on the physical and magickal properties of botanicals, such as Paul Beyerl's *Master Book of Herbalism*, before you begin. The following plants are grouped according to their magickal uses:

+ To attract love:
  Primrose, roses, pink or red clover, marjoram, jasmine, periwinkle, lemon balm, basil, marigold, daisy, orchid, anise, geranium.

+ To encourage prosperity or career success:
  Alfalfa, peppermint, spearmint, lavender, cedar, money plant, vervain, parsley.

+ For protection:
  Snapdragon, peony, verbena, valerian, anise, sage, thyme, fennel, garlic, dill, chives, ash, pussy willow, pine, basil.

⁂ To promote insight, clarity, or wisdom:
Lavender, peppermint, marigold, yarrow, anemone, apple, cornflower, elm, heather, narcissus, violets, watercress, wisteria.

You will probably want to include in your garden flowers and herbs that are associated with your sun sign, moon sign, and ascendant, as well as other prominent factors in your birthchart. If you would like to emphasize or augment certain qualities in your personality, choose plants that embody those qualities. Surrounding yourself with Aries and Leo flowers, for example, can help you become more daring or self-confident.

Gardening is an evolutionary process. Over time, the changes, needs, and personal growth you experience in your life will be reflected in your garden. Treat your garden—and the animals, birds, insects, elementals, fairies, and other entities who visit it—with respect. Nurture this conduit between yourself and the other worlds and it will nurture you in return.

Astro-Magickal Aromas

Wearing astrologically appropriate fragrances that correspond to your sign can be beneficial mentally, emotionally, and/or physically. Scented oils, perfumes, plant-enhanced waters, and resins can be applied to talismans or magickal tools to charge them. Burning incense or candles scented with astrologically related essences can establish the right mood and increase your focus during magickal work. You might also wish to bathe in water scented with specific aromatics to create the right mood before performing a magickal ritual.

In some cases, scents are connected with astrological signs in the same way as the flowers and plants from which they are extracted. Other scents have properties that relate to zo-diac signs in other ways. Musk, for example, is made from the glandular secretions of the male musk deer, so it corresponds to Scorpio, the sign that rules the sex organs.

Aries:	Bayberry, clove.
Taurus:	Bergamot, verbena, lilac.
Gemini:	Honeysuckle, lavender.
Cancer:	Lily of the valley, jasmine, rose, ginger.
Leo:	Frankincense, almond, amber.
Virgo:	Lavender, fennel.
Libra:	Peppermint, raspberry, rose.
Scorpio:	Patchouli, eucalyptus, pine, musk.
Sagittarius:	Lime, sandalwood, myrrh.
Capricorn:	Pine.
Aquarius:	Cinnamon, clove.
Pisces:	Citrus, ylang ylang, apricot, wisteria.

Metal Magick

Like gemstones, metals possess vibratory energies that have affinities with certain zodiacal signs. Gold, for example, has long been associated with the sun, the celestial body that rules Leo. (Leo is also the sign of kings, which may be why rulers often wore golden crowns.) Silver is related to the moon, and because the moon rules Cancer, it is an appropriate metal for Cancer people to wear. Metals can be combined with gemstones to increase their beneficial properties, or they may be used alone in jewelry, objets d'art, magickal tools, and other items.

Aries:	Iron, steel.
Taurus:	Copper, brass.
Gemini:	Quicksilver, mercury.
Cancer:	Silver, aluminum.
Leo:	Gold.
Virgo:	Quicksilver.
Libra:	Copper, brass.
Scorpio:	Iron, steel.
Sagittarius:	Tin.
Capricorn:	Pewter, lead.
Aquarius:	Platinum, uranium.
Pisces:	Tin, platinum.

Astro-Magickal Fabrics and Materials

The astrological correspondences inherent in fabrics and other materials can be incorporated into clothing, dream pillows, rune pouches or tarot bags, altar cloths, mojos, artwork, and other magickal accessories.

Some of the relationships between fabrics and astrological signs are obvious. Aries' symbol is the ram, so lambswool is linked with this sign; leather comes from cattle, hence its connection with Taurus, the bull. Others are based on similarities in characteristics. For example, denim, a rugged fabric, is similar to Capricorn, a sign noted for endurance, whereas silk, which is delicate and elegant, more closely mirrors Libra's qualities.

Aries:	Lambswool.
Taurus:	Leather, flax, cotton, ramie.

Gemini:	Chintz, canvas.
Cancer:	Flannel.
Leo:	Sequins, lamé, brocade.
Virgo:	Chintz, hemp, canvas.
Libra:	Silk.
Scorpio:	Snakeskin, recycled fabrics.
Sagittarius:	Rubber, spandex.
Capricorn:	Leather, mohair, cashmere, alpaca, camelhair, hemp, denim.
Aquarius:	Feathers, gauzy fabrics.
Pisces:	Rayon, nylon, acrylic.

Astro-Magickal Foods and Beverages

You've heard the expression "you are what you eat," and there's certainly a lot of truth in it. In magickal rituals, food and beverages often play a role, both for their symbolism and because they produce specific chemical reactions in the body. When you ingest something, you incorporate its energetic properties into your body. Therefore, consuming certain foods and beverages can become a part of your magickal work.

Eating foods that support or temper astrological factors in your birthchart may also be advantageous to your physical or psychological health. During a particularly difficult time in his life, a man I know felt a strong urge to eat raw sea urchins and mussels. Interestingly, his natal moon is in Cancer (symbolizing home and family), and his craving for shellfish was a subconscious way of dealing with the problems he was experiencing in his domestic situation. Hot, spicy foods such as salsa have a natural affinity with the fiery sign Aries;

coffee and tea, which stimulate mental activity, have a vibration that's similar to the mentally quick air signs Gemini and Aquarius. Some zodiacal associations are based on the principle of yin and yang. For example, sweets are considered yin foods, so they're linked with the Venus-ruled signs Taurus and Libra.

Aries:	Hot mustard, peppercorns, rhubarb, salsa, lamb, cashews, curry.
Taurus:	Dried beans, confectionery, cocoa, chocolate, wheat, spinach, beef.
Gemini:	Walnuts, hazelnuts, coffee, tea, carrots, buckwheat, caraway seeds.
Cancer:	Cheese and other dairy products, sesame oil, candied ginger, shellfish, melons.
Leo:	Almonds, sunflower seeds, yellow apples, saffron rice, gin, honey, olives.
Virgo:	Wheat, bread, honey, chicken, corn chips, popcorn, liquorice, sassafras.
Libra:	Confectionery, chocolate, strawberries, apricots, raspberries.
Scorpio:	Mushrooms, oats, rye, beer, artichokes.
Sagittarius:	Imported foods, venison, chestnuts, figs, currants, maple syrup, asparagus.
Capricorn:	Mushrooms, carob, barley, beer, potato products, poppy seeds.
Aquarius:	Coffee, ginseng, cinnamon, cloves, pomegranates.
Pisces:	Citrus fruit, peaches, water, all alcoholic beverages.

Chapter 8

Astro-Magickal Symbols

"An idea, in the highest sense of the word, cannot be conveyed but by a symbol."

—Samuel Taylor Coleridge

Symbols speak to us at an unconscious level, evoking truths, archetypes, emotions, and spiritual qualities that lie at the core of our psyches and that may not be perceived by the conscious mind. As a result, the impact symbols have on us is often quite profound, triggering deep, complex feelings. We need only observe the way patriotic people respond to their nation's flag, how Christians relate to the cross, or how Nazis reacted to the swastika to see the power of symbols at work.

We respond to symbols in collective ways as well as personal ones. Many symbols are universal, appearing in the art and artifacts of numerous cultures from different times and places. The spiral, which represents life energy, is one such symbol. In addition, each of us has a set of individual symbols that have special meanings for us alone. For me, cats signify creativity, although they may represent independence, grace, playfulness, or mystery to someone else.

Symbols aren't just handy shortcuts, like the icons for gas stations and restaurants that we see on highway signs. They are images that express the essential nature or quality of something because they also embody its essence. Historically, symbols offered one meaning for the masses and another, deeper meaning for initiates. The Star of David or Solomon's Seal is a good example. To most people, the six-pointed star is simply an image associated with the Jewish faith. But at another level, it depicts the integration of the four elements and the union between matter and spirit.

Not only can we draw symbols on paper or another surface, we can enact them physically. That's what Sufi dervishes do when they dance. Magicians illustrate symbols with their bodies and tools when they perform rituals. When a yogi forms mudras or a Catholic crosses him or herself, they are gesturing symbols. Ogham, the ancient Celtic alphabet, uses symbols derived from trees as letter equivalents, which can be signed as well as written in order to communicate.

Symbols can serve as a bridge, allowing us to make a connection with something intangible in order to incorporate it into our lives. For this reason, they play a major role in the practice of magick. When we employ symbols, we draw upon the energy of whatever they represent so we can use it for our purposes. We can also create our own symbols and project our intentions through them, which is what we do when we design sigils.

Numbers

Numbers are probably our most common and frequently utilized symbols—they're so much a part of our daily lives that we rarely think of them as symbols. Although we primarily use them as units of measurement to represent quantities, numbers also have mystical qualities that can be tapped in magickal and spiritual work. According to Rudolf Steiner, "Those who deepen themselves in what is called in the Pythagorean sense 'the study of numbers' will learn through this symbolism of numbers to understand life and the world."

In numerology, the study of numbers, each number possesses a special and unique vibration. Numbers correspond to the signs of the zodiac and the houses of an astrological chart, the sephiroth of the Kabbalistic Tree of Life, the cards in the tarot, the hexagrams in the *I Ching*, and many other mystical systems. The basic meanings of the numbers are as follows:

0: Wholeness, unity.

1: Beginnings, raw energy, individualization.

2: Association, polarity, harmony.

3: Self-expression, expansion, creativity.

4: Stability, form.

5: Change, freedom, instability.

6: Give-and-take, balance, beauty.

7: Rest, retreat, introspection.

8: Manifestation, material power.

9: Completion, bridging material and spiritual realms.

11: Inspiration, humanitarianism, universal truths.

22: Spiritual power, mastery, wisdom.

Numbers are important in magickal work because they embody energetic qualities that can be used to enhance spells, rituals, and other practices. For example, if you are doing a spell to attract money, you might want to incorporate the number eight into your magickal work. (See Chapter 11 for a prosperity spell that includes eight herbs in its ingredients.)

What's Your Number?

The date of your birth is a very important personal number, and its energy influences you throughout your lifetime. In numerology, this is often called your "life path" number, and it indicates your direction or role in this lifetime. Some numerologists consider this to be the most important number of all, and astrologers would agree.

To find your life path number, add the month, date, and year of your birth together. Keep reducing the sum by adding the digits until only a single digit remains. (Note: Usually 11 and 22, the double, or "master," numbers, are left as is rather than being reduced to the sum of their digits.)

For example, if you were born on August 21, 1958, you would figure your life number this way:

→ Add $8 + 2 + 1 + 1 + 9 + 5 + 8 = 34$.

→ Reduce the sum to a single digit by adding $3 + 4 = 7$.

Here are brief interpretations of the life roles that each number indicates:

1: Leader, initiator, pioneer, a person who breaks new ground.

2: Diplomat, mediator, agent, a go-between who assists others.

3: Artist, musician, creator, someone who brings beauty into the world.

4: Builder, artisan, technician, someone who makes practical, useful things.

5: Teacher, writer, communicator, an idea person.

6: Caretaker, homemaker, farmer, someone who nurtures and supports others.

7: Truth seeker, religious leader, philosopher, mystic, wise person.

8: Business person, manager, industrialist, a person who uses money and resources in a productive way.

9: Humanitarian, social worker, healer, a person who helps improve conditions for everyone.

11: Inventor, visionary, avatar, someone who leads by positive example.

22: A master builder who organizes people, nations, or institutions on a large scale.

Life Cycle Numbers

Our lives are never static. Indeed, change is essential for personal growth. As the planets move though the sky, they influence life on earth in many different, predictable ways. By comparing planetary movements with an individual's birth chart, an astrologer can determine what types of changes that person is likely to undergo at any given time. If we understand what cosmic influences are guiding us, we can align ourselves with them and utilize them to our advantage. (Chapter 12 discusses these cycles in detail.)

We also undergo numerological cycles, which are based on our birthdates. By working with these cycles instead of against them, we can increase our success and satisfaction in life. You'll probably notice your magickal work is more effective, too, if it is performed in harmony with the life cycles that are influencing you.

The numerological cycle known as your personal year, which changes each year, tells you which forces are operating in your life during a particular 12-month period. To determine this, add the numbers of your birth month and date to the year at your last birthday.

For example, let's say you were born on May 16 and you want to know what personal year cycle you will be experiencing from May 16, 2000 through May 15, 2001.

✤ Add 5 + 1 + 6 + 2 + 0 + 0 + 0 = 14.

✤ Reduce the sum to a single digit by adding 1 + 4 = 5.

Your personal year number for this period is five. Therefore, you'll want to try to do things that correspond to a five vibration—change your routines, travel, meet new people, learn new things. Below are suggestions for utilizing the energies each year offers.

1: This year follow your own path; assert yourself and your ideas; break new ground, plant seeds, and initiate projects that you want to see mature in the coming years.

2: This year form partnerships and work with others; patiently build toward the future; make use of opportunities; tend to small matters rather than grand ones.

3: This year enjoy friends and good times; give yourself a break and relax; be creative; travel physically and/ or mentally in order to expand your horizons and your knowledge of the world.

4: This year focus on work, money, and the material world; establish strong foundations and security; improve your health; tend to practical matters.

5: This year make changes; embrace new experiences; meet new people; promote yourself; travel; focus on communicating ideas and sharing information.

6: This year seek balance and harmony; put emphasis on home, family, and domestic life; express your love of art and beauty; nurture and give love to others.

7: This year turn inward and cultivate personal development; go on retreat or spend time alone, nurturing yourself; focus on spiritual growth rather than material success; use your intuition.

8: This year devote yourself to business, career, and financial issues; work to manifest your goals and whatever you began during the one cycle.

9: This is a year of endings, transitions, and preparation for the next cycle; eliminate anything you've outgrown to make room for new growth; examine and, if necessary, reevaluate your objectives; tie up loose ends; reap benefits and give something back.

In addition to personal year cycles, we also experience personal month cycles. We can tap the energy inherent in these shorter periods in a manner that's similar to working with personal year cycles. To find your personal month, add the number of your personal year to the number equivalent of the current month (or any month in the future that you want to know more about).

For example, if this year is a seven for you, and you want to see what March has in store,

↷ Add 7 + 3 (March's number) = 10.

↷ Reduce to a single digit by adding 1 + 0 = 1.

March is number one month for you, so during this time plan to do things that correspond to a one vibration. Use the table above that describes personal years (substituting "month" for "year") to determine how you can best utilize the energy of your personal months in both your magickal work and everyday life.

Geometric Shapes

We are influenced by the shapes existing in our environments and respond to them, even if we don't realize it consciously. Like numbers, shapes have special mystical meanings beyond their obvious ones. Artists and magicians often utilize shapes to convey deeper meanings, which are perceived intuitively. We see geometric shapes used spiritually and magickally in such ancient structures as Stonehenge and the pyramids, as well as in modern churches, mosques, and temples. Feng shui masters commonly position furnishings of specific shapes in certain areas of a home or office in order to produce desired effects; for instance, a rectangular table might be placed in the wealth/prosperity gua to stimulate growth.

Like numbers, geometric shapes can be used in magickal work to enhance the energy of a spell or ritual and to convey your intention in a symbolic manner. Whether you draw an image on a piece of parchment and include it in a mojo, wear ritual jewelry (such as a pentagram or cross) fashioned in a symbolic shape, or gesture a shape (by casting a circle or signing a blessing, for example), you invoke the power contained in that symbol and direct it for your own purposes.

Circle

Magicians usually cast a circle around themselves when performing spells, rituals, and so on (see Chapter 11 for details). This is done to provide protection and define a sacred space within which to work. The circle is a symbol of wholeness, unity, completion, and protection. Endless and self-contained, it signifies life and promise, continuity and eternity.

We automatically sense these qualities in eggs, rings, mandalas, the sun, and the full moon, which is why they are such powerful and omnipresent symbols. Our solar system itself is a giant circle; the planets move in circular orbits around the sun, and all these heavenly bodies are orbs. In a sense, time is circular, too, the seasons turning in a great wheel each year.

The circle also represents the Divine, and we see this depicted in religious art as halos around the heads of spiritual beings. Many religious structures, including ancient Greek temples, mosques, and Buddhist stupas, are circular. Stonehenge, the Temple of Athena at Delphi, St. Sepulchre's Church in Cambridge, England, and the Great Stupa at Sanchi, India are only a few examples. Others prominently feature circular elements, such as domes and rose windows, in their construction.

Square

The square symbolizes stability, permanence, solidity. All four sides are the same length, therefore, it suggests balance and equality. A square is hard to push over, which is why most buildings are squares or rectangles.

The square symbolizes the four elements as well as the four directions. In casting a circle, a magician may petition the guardians of these four directions for assistance during magickal work. We also see the square represented in the four Christian gospels, the Sufi's four gardens of Paradise, the four worlds of the Hopi, the four worlds of the Kabbalah, and the four noble truths of Buddhism. Some Hindu temples feature square mandalas, which represent earth and the principle of time, comprised of many small squares within the main square. According to A.T. Mann, "The object...is to fix and locate the temple in time and space, in relation to the sun and moon."

True squares do not exist in nature—they are human designs. Therefore, the square is emblematic of humanity's place in the cosmic scheme of things and of our imprint on earth. Leonardo da Vinci's famous drawing shows that the dimensions of the human body can be used to configure a square as well as a circle, thereby suggesting that we are the point at which the earth realm and the Divine come together.

Triangle

The triangle, with its three points, symbolizes the trinity: mind-body-spirit, father-mother-child, father-son-holy ghost, maiden-mother-crone, past-present-future, life-death-rebirth, conscious-unconscious-superconscious. We see representations of it in the three primary colors and the three dimensions of the physical world.

But although a triangle may embody wholeness, it is not static—its points are like arrows suggesting movement and direction. Mountains, with their lofty peaks pointing at the sky, are good examples of triangles existing in the natural world. Therefore, this symbol represents change, goals, dreams, growth, and the future. According to Angeles Arrien, the triangle is "associated with attainment of desired goals, and with the ability to envision new possibilities."

Triangles are used as alchemical symbols for the four elements. Upward-pointing triangles, which reach toward the heavens and spirit, represent the masculine elements fire and air; downward-pointing triangles, which aim toward the earth and matter, represent the feminine elements water and earth. The symbols for air and earth include a horizontal line through the center of the triangle. When the "male" and "female" triangles intersect, we see a geometric depiction of the union of these two energies, the merger of spirit with matter to produce life. You'll notice that this figure is also what we usually think of as the Star of David or Solomon's Seal.

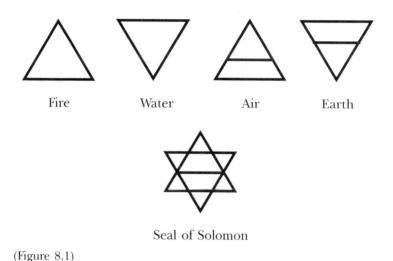

Fire   Water   Air   Earth

Seal of Solomon

(Figure 8.1)

Cross

Composed of two lines, the cross also depicts the union of spirit and matter. The vertical line, like the upward-pointing triangle, suggests movement upward and signifies spirit; the horizontal line represents the earth plane and matter. Thus the cross is yet another image of life, used as a sacred symbol by Christians, the early Celts, the Egyptians, and many others.

Like the Seal of Solomon, the Egyptian ankh and the Celtic cross also represent the union of male and female energies. The vertical line is a glyph for the male sexual organ and the circle depicts the entrance to the womb. Therefore, their connection symbolizes the merger that produces life.

Celtic Cross   Egyptian Ankh

(Figure 8.2)

From a psychological perspective, the cross signifies relationship, integration, and synthesis. We also see this depicted in the rune symbol geofu, which is usually interpreted as partnership.

In magickal work, the cross can also be used to indicate the four compass directions and the four elements. In astrology, it forms the angles—ascendant, descendant, midheaven, and imum colei—and defines the quadrants of a natal (or other) chart.

Spiral

A universal symbol of vital energy, the spiral represents the cosmic coil of life constantly renewing itself. This shape is embodied in the snake, which is itself a poignant symbol of rebirth and of the kundalini force rising up through the body from chakra to chakra. Wilhelm Reich described seeing rippling spirals of energy, which he called "orgone," in the atmosphere, and I often see them spinning above bodies of water.

Spiral

(Figure 8.3)

We can also view the spiral as a path—the path toward illumination that leads us inward and outward in search of truth. In this sense, it is similar to the labyrinth (discussed later in this chapter). This pattern often appears in Celtic and Native American art, singly or as an entwined triple spiral. Some occultists link the spiral with the third eye, the locus of psychic awareness.

According to writer Angeles Arrien, the spiral signifies "a process of coming to the same point again and again, but at a different level, so that everything is seen in a new light." It also represents movement between the planes of existence and between the different levels of our own consciousness. Magickally, this concept is enacted in the spiral dance—as the dancers move into the spiral, they experience turning inward toward the source, the womb, the Divine; as they wind out again, they return symbolically from spirit to the manifest realm.

Star or Pentagram

The five-pointed star is a representation of the human body; its points suggest the head, arms, and legs. To magicians, the pentagram is also a protection symbol, used in a variety of ways to ensure safety. It can be worn as jewelry, drawn on sigils, inscribed on candles when working spells, or signed when casting a circle.

The star also symbolizes the four elements plus spirit— the divine force that enlivens physical form. Thus, we see yet another depiction of the union of heaven and earth within ourselves.

Vesica Piscis

Created by the intersection of two interpenetrating circles, the vesica piscis symbolizes the entrance to the womb, the archetypal feminine principle. Many artists have depicted the Madonna within a vesica piscis and the Egyptians incorporated a variation of it into their cross (ankh). Seen as the union of two arcs, this image also can represent the moon.

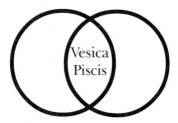

(Figure 8.4)

Platonic Solids

Plato connected the four elements with solid, geometric forms known as the Platonic Solids. According to his philosophy, the cube symbolized the earth element, the four-sided tetrahedron represented fire, the octahedron corresponded to air, and the isocahedron (which has 16 triangular sides) related to water. The dodecahedron symbolized the universe; its 12-sided surface is composed of 12 pentagons which signify the 12 signs of the zodiac.

Astrological Symbols

Sacred buildings and sites, religious art, and power objects often incorporate symbols of the heavenly bodies as a way of petitioning the gods and goddesses. As A. T. Mann says, "Each deity was associated with a particular planetary body....To evoke the god, one had to create manifestations of the cycle or numbers associated with the related luminary, planet or star."

All of the symbols for the planets contain circles or partial circles (arcs), usually in connection with crosses. This combination of geometric shapes suggests the blending of cosmic and earthly forces, the Divine working through matter, which is the essence of physical incarnation.

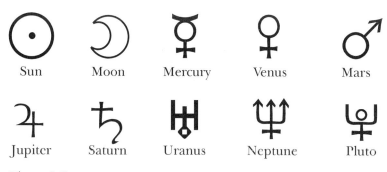

| Sun | Moon | Mercury | Venus | Mars |

| Jupiter | Saturn | Uranus | Neptune | Pluto |

(Figure 8.5)

By looking at the astrological glyphs themselves, we can discern clues to utilizing the planets' energies in our lives. For example, the sun's symbol is a circle, representing the Divine, with a dot inside, which signifies the individual. This image tells us that expressing the sun's nature involves tapping the radiant, life-giving energy of this heavenly body and focusing its creative power through the self. The moon's glyph is a crescent or partial circle. This suggests that the moon requires something else to complete it—and indeed, the moon in your birthchart plays a key role in your relationships with other people.

The horoscope pattern is a circle (symbol of wholeness and the Divine) divided by the cross of the angles (signifying matter and the physical realm). Within this, the aspects or relationships between the planets echo the essential natures of the numerological and geometric forms that comprise them. For instance, oppositions (two planets positioned opposite each other in the horoscope wheel, 180 degrees apart) signify polarity and relate to the number two. Trines (three planets configured such that each is positioned 120 degrees away from the others) form a triangle, representing creative potential and the number three.

Color Symbolism

A great deal of research has been done into the psychology of color and how we react mentally, emotionally, and physically to perceiving various hues. Studies have demonstrated that warm colors (red, orange) excite us, and can actually increase heart rate, temperature, and respiration, while cool colors (blue, green) calm us and slow our bodily responses. Chromotherapy, the art of healing with color, works by stimulating the brain (usually with colored light) to balance deficiencies or excesses and promote well-being. Rudolf Steiner designed hospitals with differently colored rooms; patients were moved from room to room as their medical conditions changed. In magickal healing work, colors are often projected via imagination to aid an ailing subject.

Swiss psychiatrist Max Lüscher found that our color preferences reveal a great deal about our personality traits and disorders. First introduced in 1947, Lüscher's color test showed that test subjects whose favorite color was dark blue wanted emotional tranquility and a calm, orderly environment. Those who liked yellow best were restless, ambitious types who sought freedom and change.

Wearing certain colors can also help you modulate your own energies or project a desired image to other people. You may have noticed that wearing blue causes you to feel more relaxed, while hot pink clothing increases your self-esteem. Purple, the color of spiritual power, frequently appears on the garments worn by Christian ministers and priests, while black, which symbolizes wholeness because it combines all hues, is a favorite of Wiccans. When performing spells or rituals, you may choose to wear colors that correspond to the nature of the magick you are doing. This can help you focus your mental/emotional energy and enhance the power of your work.

Color plays an important symbolic role in the imagery of tarot cards, which when viewed may trigger intuitive insights. We also see color used in religious, magickal, and secular art to convey subtle messages to the viewer. Certain colors are also linked with the sephiroth on the Kabbalistic Tree of Life, the seven chakras, the directions, the four elements, and the astrological signs.

Astrological Color Correspondences

Leonardo da Vinci saw colors as representations of the four elements: earth, air, fire, and water. Astrologers do too. Red, for example, is a warm, dynamic, energizing color whose vibration is akin to the fiery nature of Aries. Dark blue, the color of the ocean, is associated with the water sign Pisces.

Magick practitioners frequently utilize color in spellworking, as you'll see in Chapter 11. For example, when doing a spell to attract love, they'll burn pink candles. If they're creating talismans and amulets, they'll use pouches in astrologically appropriate colors to hold magickal ingredients. They might also drape their altars with a cloth of an appropriate color while performing a spell or ritual. Keep the following color correspondences in mind when you choose candles for spells or rituals.

Sun: Yellow, gold.

Moon: Silver, white.

Mercury: Light blue.

Venus: Pink, green.

Mars: Red.

Jupiter:	Orange.
Saturn:	Black, gray.
Uranus:	Electric blue.
Neptune:	Indigo, violet.
Pluto:	Black, maroon.
Aries:	Red, orange, russet.
Taurus:	Yellow, cream, light green.
Gemini:	Pale blue.
Cancer:	White, green, silver.
Leo:	Bright yellow, gold, orange.
Virgo:	Ocher, olive green, light brown.
Libra:	Pink, light yellow, peach.
Scorpio:	Purple, black, navy, dark red.
Sagittarius:	Orange, gold.
Capricorn:	Navy, black, gray.
Aquarius:	Cobalt blue, sky blue, fuschia.
Pisces:	Deep violet, dark blue, lavender, white.

Dream Symbolism

Ever since the beginning of time, we have wondered about the visions that fill our sleeping hours. Where do our dreams come from and what are they trying to tell us? How can the insights we receive while we sleep help us in our waking lives?

Some dream symbols—houses, death, monsters, sex, school—are familiar to most of us, and their meanings are pretty much the same for nearly everyone. However, we all have unique, personal symbols too, which have special significance for us alone. Astrological symbolism, numbers, colors, and shapes also appear with regularity in dreams; generally, their meanings are similar to those described earlier. For instance, a dream about a circle may indicate a need for unity or wholeness; a square could be advising you to establish form or permanence in your life. Frequently, two or more of these symbols will turn up in combination. When this happens, consider their relationship to each other, as well as their individual meanings.

Recurring dreams—those you have again and again—are particularly important. They usually alert you to things you need to address and may indicate whether or not you are making progress in dealing with a situation or issue. Pay special attention to dreams that occur on your birthday and those you have each month on the same date as your birthday.

Because dreams are highly personal, you are the only person who can accurately interpret your own. Keeping a journal of your dreams will help you remember them and better understand their symbolism.

Elemental Symbolism in Dreams
Fire

In a dream, fire usually represents the life force or desire. Consider the form in which fire appears and how it relates to other symbols in the dream. A cozy flame crackling in the fireplace suggests warmth, comfort, and nurturing, but a blazing inferno could mean your passions are raging out of control, especially if your house (symbol of your life) is burning up. I once dreamt that the engine of the car I was driving caught fire. Cars symbolize the body, and at the time, I was working too hard. The dream showed me that my ambition and desire for achievement, represented by fire, was damaging my health.

Because fire is also associated with purification, it might indicate areas in your life that need to be destroyed, cleansed, or rejuvenated. In some cases, fire can signify the Spirit or higher knowledge, such as the burning bush did for Moses in the wilderness.

Earth

Depending on the form it takes in your dream and its relationship to you (as well as to other dream symbols), the earth element can represent various things: your foundation (the ground under your feet), nurturing and sustenance (the land in which crops grow, Mother Earth), or physicality and the material realm. Is the earth in your dream rich and fertile? Arid and barren? Consider the way you interact with it—are you digging in the soil, slogging through mud, walking peacefully along a sandy beach? An earthquake may signify a change is coming or that you feel your position is shaky.

Air

We rarely dream about air itself. Usually, our dreams about the air element involve flying or being up in the air on a high building, a bridge, and the like. Air is related to mental activity, so if you dream you are in an airplane or soaring through the sky under your own power like a bird, it may mean you feel detached from the material realm, your body, and physical sensation. Standing at the top of a skyscraper suggests an emphasis on ideas and the intellect. Crossing a bridge over water might show you are out of touch with or avoiding your emotions. Atmospheric conditions can also represent the air element in dreams. A gentle breeze could symbolize intellectual and/or verbal adroitness or the presence of new ideas; a hurricane might indicate that you feel overwhelmed by mental demands or upset by a disturbing concept.

Because I am a mentally oriented person with lots of air signs in my birthchart, I often escape from dream monsters and other dangers by flying away. My dreams suggest that I tend to avoid dealing with real-world problems by intellectualizing them, rather than confronting them head on.

Water

A lake, river, ocean, or swimming pool in a dream represents your emotions. The condition of the water describes your own emotional state and/or how you feel about expressing emotion. Is the water clear and inviting? Or is it murky, turbulent, or cold? What is your relationship to the water? Are you swimming in it happily, letting the water buoy you up? Are you afraid to take the plunge? Do you feel you are "in over your head" or that the undertow is pulling you down? Ice or snow in a dream suggests that your emotions are cold or frozen.

Once, at the beginning of a new romance that threatened my sense of security and independence, I dreamt I was high up on a rocky cliff looking down at the sea below. I wanted to jump into the water, but the prospect of actually doing it terrified me. In this dream, the rocky cliff represented safety and stability (the earth element); my position high above the sea signified detachment and independence (air); the sea (water) symbolized the powerful and frightening emotions connected with falling (off the cliff) in love.

Dream Cycles

Our dreams often correlate to the life cycles we are experiencing at any given time. For instance, if this is a "two year" for you, you might have many dreams about partnerships; during a five year you may dream about traveling or being in school. While under the influence of a Mars transit, your dreams might be very active, vivid, or even violent. A Pluto transit could produce dreams of snakes or monsters.

By understanding the astrological and numerological cycles you are going through, you can better comprehend the significance of your dreams. As you explore dreams more extensively, you'll probably notice that your dreams follow certain patterns and cycles. These offer guidance that can be extremely valuable in your waking hours, while also helping you to get in touch with whatever cosmic influences are affecting you.

The Labyrinth: A Journey to the Center

Labyrinths are magickal circles that have been used for millennia, throughout the world, as tools for spiritual development. They can be found carved on stone walls in England and etched in Peruvian plateaus, as well as in China, Sweden, Egypt, India, Greece, and Arizona. During the Middle Ages, labyrinths were built at holy sites in Europe, the most famous being the one on the floor in France's Chartres Cathedral. Religious pilgrims traveled from one site to another to walk—or crawl—through the labyrinths.

A labyrinth is a single, winding pathway of concentric curves or circuits that ultimately leads to the center and back out again. Walking it symbolizes the journey to your own center or to the Source. Two labyrinth designs predominate today. The seven-circuit design, which emphasizes balance between humanity and nature, is favored by Pagans and other followers of earth-centered spiritual traditions. The 11-circuit design from the Chartres Cathedral, which the Knights Templars may have introduced into Europe after the Crusades, emerged with the development of Christianity and symbolizes the evolution of the human community.

Seven Circuit Labyrinth

Chartres-style Labyrinth

(Figure 8.6)

Unlike mazes, which are puzzles with many blind alleys, labyrinths are magickal, curved, single-path systems for enhancing intuition and transformation. You cannot get lost in a labyrinth and you can always see where you are going, whereas a maze is designed to confuse and confound you.

(The famous Cretan prison of Greek mythology, where the minotaur lived, was really a maze, not a labyrinth.)

Labyrinths can be made of just about anything—built from stone, drawn on cardboard or cloth, cut into turf, or fashioned with masking tape, yarn, sticks, feathers, or whatever materials are available. The Chinese used lighted incense to form the design. I sometimes trace the symbol in the sandy beaches on the island where I live. Sig Lonegren (author of *Labyrinths: Ancient Myths and Modern Uses*) has even configured them with fire.

Many people use labyrinths as a form of walking meditation; they say the process makes them feel relaxed or centered. I consider my labyrinth to be a sacred space in which I not only meditate, but do spiritual and magickal work as well. A labyrinth is also a powerful sending and receiving device that focuses, amplifies, and transmits energies. Thoughts, feelings, visualizations, and incantations become more powerful and can be projected outward with greater facility from the labyrinth's center. And because the mind is more peaceful within the labyrinth, receiving messages from spiritual entities, elementals, or other people becomes easier while you're inside one.

Although most labyrinths are intended to be walked, some people find that an altered state of consciousness can be achieved by simply running a finger through the circuits of an illustration—a good example of how a symbol is equivalent to the actual object it depicts. Try it yourself and see.

Labyrinth Ritual

The circuits of the seven-circuit labyrinth correspond to the seven main chakras, the seven tones of the musical scale, the seven colors of the visible spectrum, and the seven "original" bodies in our solar system—which may explain why labyrinths balance our energy fields.

This ritual, which fellow writers/metaphysicians Sig Lonegren and Steven McFadden shared with me, is designed to help you get in touch with astrological energies and their operations in your life.

Labyrinth Ritual

(Figure 8.7)

1. Choose seven people to represent the sun, moon, Mercury, Venus, Mars, Jupiter, and Saturn. It's more dramatic and colorful if they dress up in costumes or masks that convey the essence of the planet or luminary's energy, so use your imagination!

2. Position each person at the entrance to the circuit that corresponds to his/her planet or luminary (see figure 8.7). If the labyrinth isn't big enough for this, they can stand outside the circle and move to the entrance of the related circuit as the walker approaches.

3. Begin walking through the labyrinth. (It's best if only one person walks it at a time.) As you come to the entrance of a circuit, the "planet" calls out a word that relates to that planet's nature. For instance, as you approach the Mars circuit, the person representing Mars might say "action" or "assertiveness." When you reach the entrance to Saturn's circuit, that "planet" could say "discipline," "responsibility," or "structure."

4. As you walk through each planet's circuit, contemplate the meaning of the keyword associated with that planet and what it implies in your own life.

5. On the way into the center of the labyrinth, reflect on how each planet's energy works within you and affects you personally. Consider ways in which you respond to the planet's influence, how you actualize it in your life, and any difficulties you have with it.

6. On the way out of the labyrinth, contemplate how you use each planet's energy in the outer world, in your interactions with other people, in your work, how it challenges you, and ways you might be able to handle it better.

7. Continue until each person has had a chance to walk through the labyrinth.

8. If you wish, share insights with each other afterwards.

Chapter 9

Timing Magickal Work

"To every thing there is a season, and a time to every purpose under the heaven."

—Ecclesiastes 3:1

If you plant tomatoes in Vermont in June, your chances of reaping a bountiful harvest are significantly better than if you plant them in March. Likewise, your magickal work has a better chance of bearing fruit if you sow the seeds at the proper time, when cosmic energies are in sync with your intentions.

Life on earth is cyclic—we exist in a pattern of daily, monthly, and yearly cycles. The birthchart itself is a circle through which we experience the cyclic motions of the planets and the corresponding events in our lives. These cycles provide a framework upon which we can build, an energy system that we can draw from to fuel our magickal operations.

Lunar Cycles

It's easy to see how the moon's phases affect earthly affairs. During full moons, the tides are generally higher than at other times of the month, more babies are born, and more crimes of passion are committed. Many people feel energetic or stimulated when the moon is full. Conversely, new moons tend to be low-energy periods when we are less vigorous or enthusiastic.

Whether your objectives are mundane or magickal, your efforts are more likely to succeed if you coordinate them with the moon's cycles.

New Moon

The new moon initiates a cycle of endings and beginnings. Try to wind up any pending business or activities before the new moon, then initiate new ones that you want to grow after the moon begins to wax again. Because the new moon is a low-energy period, this is a good time to rest, meditate, or retreat from outer-world activities.

In magickal work

When the moon is new, do magick that involves endings or things you wish to remain secret. Invisibility spells should be performed during the dark of the moon. Banishing rites and spells to dissolve ties are strengthened by this lunar phase. Some people experience an increase in their intuitive abilities during this time; others have precognitive or particularly meaningful dreams.

Waxing Moon

The waxing moon promotes growth. Therefore, this is a good period to begin new ventures or projects that involve increase. If you're starting a business or new job, adding on to your home, beginning a family, or writing a symphony, this is an opportune time to do it. As the moon grows, so will your endeavors.

In magickal work

During the waxing moon, do magick to encourage growth. Prosperity spells, love spells, fertility spells, blessings for a new home or business, planting/gardening rituals, spells to attract friends or to increase artistic creativity will be enhanced by the energy of this lunar phase.

Full Moon

The full moon brings to fruition things that were initiated around the new moon (or earlier). The glow of the full moon sheds light on situations, so you can see what's happening. It also brings to light matters that may have been hidden or unclear before.

In magickal work

On the full moon, perform magick that involves culmination or illumination. Some people feel the full moon is a time when occult knowledge is more accessible and that it is therefore a particularly good time to do divination or scrying. Marriage rites and celebrations to honor accomplishments or harvests are also in harmony with this lunar phase.

Waning Moon

The waning moon assists decrease. This two-week period is an advantageous time to do things that involve reduction: start a diet, clean out closets, pay bills, prune shrubs, or end a relationship. As the moon's light decreases, so will whatever you begin at this time. During this period, you can also refine projects or systems, follow up on matters you initiated during the waxing moon, and make repairs.

In magickal work

During the waning moon, do magick that involves decrease. Spells to bind an enemy, break a bond, curb desires, or eliminate an unwanted habit or attitude will benefit from the energy of this lunar phase.

The Celestial Week

In earlier times, it was believed that each of the then-known bodies in our solar system presided over a day of the week. The names given to the days reflect this rulership.

Sunday:	Sun
Monday:	Moon
Tuesday:	Mars (Tir is the Norse equivalent of Mars.)
Wednesday (Mercredi in French):	Mercury
Thursday:	Jupiter (Thor is the Norse equivalent of Jupiter.)
Friday:	Venus (Freya is the Norse equivalent of Venus.)
Saturday:	Saturn

You can invoke the energy of a particular planet or luminary to aid your magickal work by performing spells and rituals on the day that corresponds to that heavenly body. Work spells whose objectives are in harmony with the nature of the planet or light. (See Chapter 4 for more information about the planets.)

Sunday: Do magick to strengthen your self-esteem, personal power, or public image, advance your career, bless a business venture, enhance creativity, or improve health and vitality.

Monday: Do magick to protect home and/or family, increase fertility, aid female health problems, provide security, balance emotions, or improve intuition.

Tuesday: Do magick to bolster courage, augment physical strength and vitality, increase sexual desire or potency, or overcome challenges.

Wednesday: Do magick to increase mental powers, facilitate communication with other people or nonphysical entities, provide protection and ease when traveling, negotiate business deals and contracts, or improve relationships with siblings or neighbors.

Thursday: Do magick to enhance prosperity, increase higher knowledge, expand opportunities in business or personal areas, provide protection and ease when traveling long distances, reinforce health and vitality, attract success in legal matters, or for general good luck.

Friday: Do magick to increase prosperity, attract a lover or improve an existing relationship, enhance friendships and social situations, spark creativity, or gain the support of helpful people.

Saturday: Do magick to bind an enemy, set boundaries, restrict growth, provide protection, establish stable foundations, bring about endings, increase discipline and willpower, or eliminate unwanted habits.

Planetary Hours

Each planet or luminary also rules certain hours of the day. The period between sunset and sunrise is divided into 12 equal portions, as is the period between sunset and sunrise. (For ease of calculation, some people simply align the planets with the hours according to clock time.) The first "hour" of the day is governed by the heavenly body that rules the day—the sun on Sunday, the moon on Monday, and so forth. Subsequent hours are presided over in the following sequence: sun, Venus, Mercury, moon, Saturn, Jupiter, Mars, and the cycle continues in this sequence until the next sunrise.

For example, on Monday, the moon rules the first hour, Saturn the second, Jupiter the third, and so on. On Thursday, Jupiter's influence dominates during the first hour, Mars' during the second, the sun's during the third, and so on.

This system of division allows you to refine your magickal work and blend planetary energies to suit your purposes. Many spells and rituals incorporate qualities of more than one heavenly body; for instance, both Venus and Jupiter can enhance prosperity spells. Therefore, you could perform a money spell during the fourth hour on Thursday or the fifth hour on Friday in order to take advantage of the favorable energies of both planets. A spell to strengthen a marriage could benefit from combining the energies of Venus and the moon; a spell to increase sexual passion in a love relationship might be done under the influences of both Venus and Mars. (See Table of Planetary Hours on page 137.)

By "mixing and matching" celestial energies, you can draw upon whatever forces you need. First determine which of the heavenly bodies relate(s) to your intention. Generally speaking, you'll want to consider the sun's sign position as most important, then the moon's phase and sign, then the day of the week, then the planetary hour. However, if you are

Table of Planetary Hours

	Sunday	Monday	Tuesday	Wednesday	Thursday	Friday	Saturday
1st Hour	Sun	Moon	Mars	Mercury	Jupiter	Venus	Saturn
2nd Hour	Venus	Saturn	Sun	Moon	Mars	Mercury	Jupiter
3rd Hour	Mercury	Jupiter	Venus	Saturn	Sun	Moon	Mars
4th Hour	Moon	Mars	Mercury	Jupiter	Venus	Saturn	Sun
5th Hour	Saturn	Sun	Moon	Mars	Mercury	Jupiter	Venus
6th Hour	Jupiter	Venus	Saturn	Sun	Moon	Mars	Mercury
7th Hour	Mars	Mercury	Jupiter	Venus	Saturn	Sun	Moon
8th Hour	Sun	Moon	Mars	Mercury	Jupiter	Venus	Saturn
9th Hour	Venus	Saturn	Sun	Moon	Mars	Mercury	Jupiter
10th Hour	Mercury	Jupiter	Venus	Saturn	Sun	Moon	Mars
11th Hour	Moon	Mars	Mercury	Jupiter	Venus	Saturn	Sun
12th Hour	Saturn	Sun	Moon	Mars	Mercury	Jupiter	Venus

(Figure 9.1)

doing a fertility spell, the moon's position will take precedence. If you are doing magick to get a job while the sun is in Aquarius and time is a factor, you might decide to overrule the sun's sign (unless the job you're seeking is in an Aquarian field, such as computers, aviation, or astrology) and perform a spell or ritual during the waxing moon, on Sunday, during the sixth (Jupiter's) hour of the day.

As you become more familiar with the basic natures of the planets and luminaries, as well as the signs they rule, you'll be able to design spells and rituals that successfully utilize cosmic energies to produce positive results. Chapter 12 provides information about planetary cycles and how they affect mundane and magickal matters.

Chapter 10

The Magician's Toolbox

"Magic...uses all of reality,
the world itself, as its medium."

—Bill Whitcomb

Like skilled practitioners in any other line of work, magicians employ various tools of the trade to help focus, strengthen, and otherwise aid their endeavors. Strictly speaking, none of these tools is necessary to perform magick spells or rituals. But they can help "set the stage" and create an atmosphere that's conducive to working magick. In this sense, magick is a little like lovemaking—mood and environment do count and can influence the experience as well as the outcome.

You can fabricate your own magickal implements or purchase them in occult/new age stores. In either case, you'll need to cleanse, consecrate, and charge your tools before you use them. The process of creating these tools is a magickal act and it should be done with reverence within a sacred space. Each time you perform magick with them, their powers will increase. When they are not in use, your tools should be carefully stored to protect them. Metaphysical shops sell ready-made pouches of various sizes and materials that are designed for this purpose. I wrap mine in silk, then place them in a special box. It's not a good idea to let other people handle or work magick with your tools because these sensitive devices retain the vibrations of everything they touch.

The four basic tools of magick are illustrated in the suits of the tarot: wands, swords, pentacles, and cups. Most magicians also use other equipment, including candles, incense, cauldrons, pendulums, runes, tarot cards, gemstones and crystals, bells, robes, magick mirrors, figurines of favorite gods and goddesses, herbs, oils, various talismans, and a grimoire, or "book of shadows," in which spells are recorded. Choose whichever implements you prefer and feel will be assets to you in your magickal work.

Wand

The magick wand is the most familiar and arguably the most utilized tool in the magician's toolbox (though not necessarily for followers of Wicca). Contrary to images in movies and fairytales, it is not used to turn people into toads or to make them disappear. A magician may cast circles with a wand or direct his/her own energy toward specific objectives with it. Used to invoke cosmic energies during rituals and spellworking, the wand enables the magician to draw down power from the spiritual realm and focus it in the manifest world.

The wand embodies the fire element, signifying will, creativity, action, desire, spirit, individuality, and courage. It is associated with masculine power (its phallic symbolism is obvious), summer, the south, the sun's energy, and the heart. Often made of wood, the wand also has an affinity with trees (especially in Celtic/Druid traditions), which tarot cards often depict.

If you decide to make your own magick wand, do it when the sun and moon are in fire signs (Aries, Leo, Sagittarius) and during the days and hours that correspond to the sun, Mars, or Jupiter (see Chapter 9). The Spring Equinox and Summer Solstice are ideal times to fashion this magickal device.

Cut a slender branch about 10 to 12 inches long from an ash, oak, holly, hazel, willow, rowan, apple, yew, or elder tree. (Remember to thank the tree!) Trim off small shoots and bark, then sand it smooth—or leave it in its natural condition if you prefer. You can also fabricate a magick wand from a plain wooden dowel with a decorative finial glued on one end.

Decorate your wand in a manner that bespeaks fire energy. Paint it red or orange, perhaps with flames rising up its sides; paint the finial so that it resembles a flame. A traditional design divides the shaft into three equal segments, using rings of yellow to separate the three red sections, with three flame-shaped Yods (Hebrew letters) painted on the tip.

Draw the glyphs for Aries, Leo, Sagittarius, the sun, Mars, and/or Jupiter on the stalk; illustrate it with sigils (see pages 151-159); carve upward-pointing triangles in it; write the names of angels such as Michael, Gabriel, Raphael, and/or others whose assistance you wish to invoke, your own magickal name, or words of power on it using a magickal alphabet; draw the hexagram for "Ch'ien" from the *I Ching* on it—use whatever symbols speak to you. You may also wish to affix "fire" gemstones (diamond, bloodstone, ruby, amber, tiger eye, carnelian, or topaz) to your wand or wrap it with gold or iron bands. Some people adorn their wands with feathers, spirit animal symbolism, and other talismanic materials or images that have personal significance for them. I encourage you to use your imagination, rather than merely following rules set down by a secret order or tradition.

Charging Your Magick Wand

Before you use your wand to work magick, you'll want to infuse it with personal and elemental energy in order to transform it from an ordinary stick of wood (or other material) into a magickal tool. First, cast a circle (see Chapter 11). Next, cleanse the wand physically with water and mentally by envisioning it surrounded and suffused with pure white light. I also recommend purifying it with smoke, either from specially chosen incense, a sage smudge stick, or a fire made from ash, birch, oak, holly, hazel, willow, rowan, apple, yew, and/or elder woods.

Then, anoint your wand with oil or resin of bayberry, clove, frankincense, almond, sandalwood, or myrrh. When you have finished, walk to the south corner of your room or property, hold the wand up toward the sun, and state aloud an affirmation such as "I now consecrate this wand to do the work of the God/Goddess and charge it to assist me in my magickal practice, in harmony with Divine Will, my own true will, and for the good of all concerned."

Some magicians charge ritual tools by bringing them into contact with all four elements: water, earth (salt), fire, and air (incense). However, salt can corrode metal and fire applied directly will burn wood. More elaborate rituals can be designed to further enhance the charging process. You'll find consecration rituals outlined in *The Golden Dawn* by Israel Regardie, *Modern Magick* by Donald Michael Kraig, *Secrets of a Witch's Coven* by Morwyn, and other books on magick.

I hung my wand from an apple tree in the south corner of my yard for the solar month of Leo. Then I walked through my labyrinth with it each day for a lunar month while chanting the above affirmation and visualizing the sun's power permeating it. Finally I charged it with my own blood, sweat, and tears. (Semen may also be used to charge a magick wand, in keeping with the tool's creative, masculine nature.) Once again, the most important factor is your intention, so employ whatever ceremony or procedure will enable you to direct your mental powers for your purposes.

Athame

The athame, a double-edged ritual dagger, corresponds to the element of air, representing thought, communication, the breath of life, and the power of light over darkness. It is connected with masculine power (like the wand's, its phallic symbolism is obvious), spring, the East, Mercury and Uranus, and the mind.

Although followers of Wicca may cast circles with their athames, other magicians consider it a banishing tool. Before performing a ritual, use it to clear away any harmful, disruptive, or unbalanced energies from your sacred space. It can also disperse negativity and aid you in working protection or banishing spells. Your ritual dagger should not be used to cut herbs or food or for other mundane purposes, although you may cut the wood for your magick wand with it, if you wish.

You can purchase an athame from an occult store or fabricate your own if you possess jewelry-making or smithing skills. Some magicians prefer antique athames, however, you should know how a tool was used in the past before you employ it yourself, for it retains energies generated by previous owners and acts. Some people believe the blade should never have drawn blood, though I know one magician whose athame was consecrated in a sacred ritual of taking a deer and charged with the deer's blood as well as his own.

If you decide to make your own ritual dagger, do it when the sun and moon are in air signs (Gemini, Libra, Aquarius) and during the days and hours that correspond to Mercury. Imbolc and the Autumn Equinox are ideal times to fashion this magickal device.

The blade of an athame is normally about four to six inches long and fitted into a hilt that rests comfortably in your hand. Usually, the hilt is made of wood, leather, or metal and painted either black or the "air" colors blue and yellow. I suggest decorating the hilt with symbols of the air element, such as the upward-pointing triangle with a horizontal line through its center, or the glyphs for Gemini, Libra, Aquarius, Mercury, and/or Uranus. Illustrate it with sigils (see below), words of power or angelic names, runes, or hexagrams from the *I Ching*—whichever symbols appeal to you. You might also wish to affix gemstones to your athame to attract the air element—aquamarine, clear quartz, agate, lapis lazuli, garnet, or zircon—or form the blade of copper or brass, which are air metals.

Charging Your Athame

Before you use your dagger to work magick, you'll want to infuse it with personal and elemental energy in order to transform it from an ordinary knife into a magickal implement. After casting a circle (see Chapter 11), cleanse your athame physically with water and mentally by envisioning it surrounded and suffused with pure white light. I also recommend purifying it with smoke, either from specially chosen incense, a sage smudge stick, or a fire made from ash, birch, oak, holly, hazel, willow, rowan, apple, yew, and/or elder woods.

Then, anoint your athame with honeysuckle, lavender, peppermint, raspberry, rose, cinnamon, or clove oil. When you have finished, walk to the east corner of your room or property, hold the athame up toward the sky, and state aloud an affirmation such as "I now consecrate this athame to do the work of the God/Goddess and charge it to assist me in my magickal practice, in harmony with Divine Will, my own true will, and for the good of all concerned." You may design a more elaborate ritual to consecrate and charge your dagger if you wish, or you can refer to other books on magick for suggestions.

Pentagram/Pentacle

Representative of the element of earth, the five-pointed star known as the pentagram or pentacle is associated with feminine power, winter, the north, the earth, and the human body. The earth element is connected with fertility, stability, endurance, practical matters, the material world, and the embodiment of spirit within the manifest realm.

Pentagrams are symbols of protection and are often worn during magickal rituals to ensure safety while working between the worlds. A pentagram may also be placed on an altar for this purpose and magicians frequently sign them in the air when casting a circle. I sometimes paint them on my body to lend protection during rites.

Unless you are skilled in jewelry-making, you'll probably purchase your pentagram from an occult/new age store. (Of course, you could fabricate one from something other than metal—cloth, wood, cardboard, just about any material will suffice, as the symbol itself is what's important.) Some pentagrams are decorated with other magickal imagery, including spirals, circles, infinity symbols, Hebrew letters, planetary glyphs, and so on—you can add these yourself if you wish. Because I am of Irish ancestry, I chose one that is encircled with Celtic knots. You may prefer one with gemstones appropriate to the earth element: emerald, star sapphire, turquoise, jade, peridot, pink jasper, onyx, jet, smoky quartz, or malachite.

Charging Your Pentagram

Before you begin wearing your pentagram, you'll want to infuse it with personal and elemental energy in order to transform it into a magickal tool. It's best to do this when the sun and moon are in earth signs (Taurus, Virgo, Capricorn) and during the days and hours that correspond to Venus.

Beltane is an ideal time to prepare your pentagram. After casting a circle, cleanse your pentagram physically with water and mentally by envisioning it surrounded and suffused with pure white light. I also recommend purifying it with smoke, either from specially chosen incense, a sage smudge stick, or a fire made from ash, birch, oak, holly, hazel, willow, rowan, apple, yew, and/or elder woods.

Then, anoint your pentagram with bergamot, verbena, lilac, lavender, fennel, or pine oil. When you have finished, walk to the north corner of your room or property, hold the pentagram in your outstretched hand, and state aloud an affirmation, such as "I now consecrate this pentagram to do the work of the God/Goddess and charge it to assist me in my magickal practice, in harmony with Divine Will, my own true will, and for the good of all concerned."

If you prefer, you may design a more elaborate ritual to consecrate and charge your pentagram or refer to other books on magick for suggestions. For example, after anointing my pentagram during the new moon in Taurus, I wrapped it in silk, placed it in a leather box, and buried it in the ground beneath my labyrinth for one lunar month. I did this to further imbue my pentagram with earth energy and the feminine power of the moon in all her phases. Because a labyrinth can be used to amplify and intensify a magician's intentions, I use mine to charge, focus, and empower nearly all of my magickal operations.

Chalice

The chalice or cup is a symbol of the water element, representing love, intuition, fertility, nurturing, compassion, and security. It is associated with feminine power (its vaginal symbolism is obvious), autumn, the west, the moon, and the womb.

Chalices are used to hold liquids during rituals; however, you should not drink from your chalice except for magickal purposes. Your chalice may be made of glass, metal, ceramic, or wood. I prefer silver (or silverplate) because this tool is linked with the moon. If you wish, you can decorate your chalice with pearls or moonstones (gems that correspond to the moon) and paint or engrave it with magickal imagery—the glyph for the moon, a downward-pointing triangle, sigils, words of power or angelic names, runes, or hexagrams from the *I Ching*. In the tradition of the Golden Dawn, the bowl of the chalice is painted to resemble a crocus flower, with blue petals and orange inscriptions. (Note: Make sure to use lead-free paint.)

Charging Your Chalice

Before you use your chalice, you'll want to infuse it with personal and elemental energy in order to transform it from an ordinary cup into a magickal tool. It's best to do this when the sun and moon are in water signs (Cancer, Scorpio, Pisces) and during the days and hours that correspond to the moon. The Summer Solstice and Samhain are also good times to charge your chalice. After casting a circle, cleanse your chalice physically with water and mentally by envisioning it surrounded and suffused with pure white light. I also recommend purifying it with smoke, either from specially chosen incense, a sage smudge stick, or a fire made from ash, birch, oak, holly, hazel, willow, rowan, apple, yew, and/or elder woods.

Then, anoint your chalice with the liquid from lily of the valley, jasmine, or rose stems and petals (don't put lily of the valley near the rim of the bowl, as this flower is toxic). Oils or flower essences that contain infusions of these plants will work, too. When you have finished, walk to the west corner of your room or property, hold the chalice in your outstretched hand, and state aloud an affirmation, such as, "I now consecrate this chalice to do the work of the God/Goddess and charge it to assist me in my magickal practice, in harmony with Divine Will, my own true will, and for the good of all concerned."

If you prefer, you may design a more elaborate ritual to consecrate and charge your chalice. For example, before rubbing my chalice with jasmine and rose oils, I submerged it in a body of water that is special to me for one lunar month to enhance the feminine energies of the water element and the moon.

Other Magickal Tools

Magicians often utilize other tools in their practices, too. The sword is a fire weapon, used to banish harmful or disruptive influences from a sacred space. This powerful masculine symbol is frequently associated with the avenging angel Michael and wielded in ceremonies or rituals.

Cauldrons are convenient for holding water, herbal mixtures, or magickal brews during rituals. When the sun and/or moon is in Virgo (sign of the hearth), decorate this feminine tool with the glyph for Mercury, runes, sigils, or symbols that appeal to you.

Incense is one of the most common and innocent-looking magickal tools, but don't let its unassuming form fool you—it can be very powerful. Magicians burn incense to purify sacred space and to carry messages or prayers to deities in the higher realms. Its aromatic properties also help stimulate the senses and the brain to enhance concentration.

Bells represent feminine energy. They are used to punctuate meditation, prayers, or chanting, to mark turning points in rituals, and to attract the attention of deities. Cords and ribbons may be knotted with spells (see Chapter 11). Crystal balls and magick mirrors are used for scrying; runes, tarot cards, and pendulums are popular divination tools.

Candles

Many spells and rituals involve burning candles. Indeed, candle magick is so common and widespread that whole books are devoted to the subject. Candles symbolize the light of spirit, truth, and wisdom shining through the darkness of ignorance and fear. Putting candles on a birthday cake for the purpose of making a wish is a simple form of candle magick. So is the practice of lighting candles for novenas.

Choose candles in colors that correspond to your intentions: pink or red for love, green or gold for prosperity, white for protection, purple for power or success, blue for peace and insight, black for banishing. (See Chapter 8 for more information about color.) Before lighting a candle for spellworking, wash and dry it to remove any unwanted vibrations. With a sharp implement, cut words or designs in the wax that describe your purpose. For example, if your objective is to attract money, you might carve "abundance" or "prosperity" or engrave a sigil for these words directly into the candle. Then rub it with oil scented with an astrologically appropriate fragrance (see Chapter 7).

As the candle burns, your intention is carried as a thoughtform in the smoke to the spirit world. The energy generated influences the nonphysical realm in order to produce desired changes here on earth. Allow the candle to burn down completely—do not blow it out. If you must extinguish the flame before the candle has burned itself out, use a snuffer or wet your fingers and pinch it out instead.

Candle Ritual to Attract Love

You'll need two red or rose-colored taper candles for this simple but powerful ritual. If you know feng shui, perform the ritual in the relationship gua of your home or bedroom.

The best time to do this ritual is on Friday, one week before the full moon, preferably when the sun and/or moon is in Taurus or Libra.

1. Cast a circle (see Chapter 11).

2. Relax, put your mind at ease, and focus all your attention on the project before you.

3. With a sharp instrument, carve words such as "love," "passion," "joy"—whatever you want your relationship to bring—on the two candles.

4. Fit the candles into holders and place them about a foot apart.

5. Light the candles, and as they burn, repeat an affirmation such as "I now attract a lover who is right for me in every way" three times. (Note: Do not stipulate who that lover will be, as doing so is manipulative and may prevent the right person from coming into your life.)

6. Allow the candles to burn for at least one hour. During this period, you may remain inside the circle or cut a doorway in it to go out, leaving the candles burning inside the circle. (Note: As a safety precaution, don't go away from home while the candles are still lit.)

7. After an hour or so, extinguish the candles with a snuffer or by wetting your fingers and pinching out the flame—don't blow them out.

8. Open the circle and thank the deities who have assisted you in your spellworking.

Repeat this ritual every day until the moon is full. Each day, move the candles closer together until, on the day of the full moon, they are touching. The last time you perform this ritual, allow the candles to finish burning completely before extinguishing them.

Grimoire

Also known as a book of shadows, a grimoire is your personal collection of spells. It contains your own secret recipes, along with information about the purposes for which you employed these spells, what you experienced in the process, and the results you obtained. In my grimoire, I also record the dates when certain spells were performed and relevant astrological data (lunar phases, solar positions, planetary patterns), along with explanations of how celestial energies contributed to the spellworking.

Some people believe you shouln't allow anyone else to read your grimoire. I feel it's okay to share my secrets with a magickal partner or someone I trust, and I consider the exchange of occult knowledge—when done responsibly and selectively—to be healthy. For this reason, I chose from my own book of shadows some spells and rituals that I feel will be useful and safe for readers to perform, and have included them in this book. A grimoire should never be made accessible to those who might misuse or misunderstand its contents.

As you progress in your magickal work, you may amend some of your earlier methods or ingredients. Most likely, you'll gain greater understanding of the spells you did in the beginning stages and why they were—or were not—successful. Remember to include mistakes or failures, as these can be helpful, too.

Sigils

The subconscious mind responds more readily to symbols and images than to words. However, words of power, incantations, and affirmations play an important role in magickal work. One way to impress messages on your subconscious, thereby increasing the effectiveness of your affirmations, is to transform written words into pictures, called sigils.

A sigil (from the Latin sigillum, meaning sign) is a symbol you create to embody a specific intention. It is also a secret message to yourself, which no one else can interpret. A sigil may consist of letters, numbers, planetary glyphs, geometric shapes, and/or other magickal designs. Like any other true symbol, it contains the essence of a word, phrase, prayer, mantra, and so on within its pattern.

Sigils drawn on parchment are often placed in talismans and amulets. I frequently include them in my magickal artwork and sometimes paint them on my body for ritual purposes. I even know people who have sigils as tattoos. The creation of a sigil is a magickal process, therefore you'll want to relax, clear your mind, establish a conducive environment, and perhaps cast a circle before you start.

Although the possibilities are limited only by your imagination, an easy technique for fashioning a sigil is to collapse or condense letters into an image. Begin by writing your desire in the form of an affirmation, meaning a simple, unambiguous, positive statement. Remember to word your intention in the present tense, so your subconscious knows you want it to take effect now, rather than at some unspecified time in the future. Let's use one of my favorite, all-purpose affirmations—"I am healthy, happy, and fulfilled on every level"—as an example.

Print the affirmation in capital letters. Next, cross out all the duplicate letters, leaving: IAMHELTYPNDFUOVR. Some people also eliminate all the vowels (a practice derived from the Hebrew tradition), which reduces the number of letters you must configure and makes the design process easier. Now your affirmation consists of: MHLTPNDFVR.

Here's where you get to be creative. The objective is to entwine the letters, forming a design that you find pleasing. You can use simple, block letters or decorative cursive ones, depending on your preference. You can overlay the letters, one on top of another. You can stack them, invert them, reverse them, or turn them on their sides. You can draw some of the letters large and some small. You can combine upper and lowercase letters—it's completely up to you.

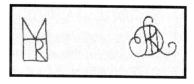

(Figure 10.1)

Place your finished sigil where you will see it often. Each time you look at it, your subconscious will be reminded of the intention behind it. Or, incorporate it into a talisman, spell, or ritual.

Using Sigils in Meditation

Sigils can also be used as focal points for meditation and contemplation. It's usually best to choose a single word that describes a particular quality you desire, such as "compassion" or "courage" or "patience" for your sigil.

Before you create the sigil, remember a situation in which you experienced this condition in your own life and allow yourself to revisit the feelings you had at that time. The more vividly you can relive this experience in your mind, the better. Hold onto this feeling while you draw your sigil, using the condensed alphabet method outlined above, and project the emotion into your design. Your memory and its emotional content are fused into the sigil, which acts as a prompt for your subconscious.

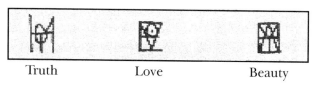

Truth   Love   Beauty

(Figure 10.2)

Each time you look at the sigil during meditation or contemplation, you absorb its energy. The quality with which the sigil is imbued will gradually impress itself on you and become more fully present in your life.

Creating a Sigil on a Magick Square

A magick square is an ancient configuration of smaller, numbered squares arranged in rows and columns in such a way that the numbers in each column and row add up to the same sum. Called kamea in Hebrew, these squares equate with the sephiroth on the Kabbalistic Tree of Life and possess magickal properties.

There are many kinds of magick squares. The following ones correspond to the sun, moon, and the five planets that can be seen with the naked eye. These squares embody the energies of the celestial bodies and can be used to attract cosmic forces for magickal purposes.

6	32	3	34	35	1
7	11	27	28	8	30
19	14	16	15	23	24
18	20	22	21	17	13
25	29	10	9	26	12
36	5	33	4	2	31

Sun

(Figure 10.3)

37	78	29	70	21	62	13	54	5
6	38	79	30	71	22	63	14	46
47	7	39	80	31	72	23	55	15
16	48	8	40	81	32	64	24	56
57	17	49	9	41	73	33	65	25
26	58	18	50	1	42	74	34	66
67	27	59	10	51	2	43	75	35
36	68	19	60	11	52	3	44	76
77	28	69	20	61	12	53	4	45

Moon

22	47	16	41	10	35	4
5	23	48	17	42	11	29
30	6	24	49	18	36	12
13	31	7	25	43	19	37
38	14	32	1	26	44	20
21	39	8	33	2	27	45
46	15	40	9	34	3	28

Venus

(Figure 10.3 continued)

8	58	59	5	4	62	63	1
49	15	14	52	53	11	10	56
41	23	22	44	45	19	18	48
32	34	35	29	28	38	39	25
40	26	27	37	36	30	31	33
17	47	46	20	21	43	42	24
9	55	54	12	13	51	50	16
64	2	3	61	60	6	7	57

Mercury

11	24	7	20	3
4	12	25	8	16
17	5	13	21	9
10	18	1	14	22
23	6	19	2	15

Mars

4	9	2
3	5	7
8	1	6

Saturn

4	14	15	1
9	7	6	12
5	11	10	8
16	2	3	13

Jupiter

(Figure 10.3 continued)

1	2	3	4	5	6	7	8	9
A	B	C	D	E	F	G	H	I
J	K	L	M	N	O	P	Q	R
S	T	U	V	W	X	Y	Z	

Number/Letter Table

(Figure 10.4)

One way to tap the power of a planet or luminary is to draw a sigil on its magick square.

1. Choose the magick square that relates to the planet that rules your intent. Let's say your objective is to develop inner strength. Strength is considered to be a Saturnian quality.

2. Translate the letters in the keyword for your intention to their numerological values (see figure 10.4).

    S T R E N G T H

    1 2 9 5 5 7 2 8

3. Lay a sheet of tracing paper over the magick square.

4. Find the numbered square that corresponds to the numerological equivalent of your first letter (s = 1) and draw a small circle in the square. Then draw a line from that circle to the numbered square for the second letter value (t = 2), and so on until the word has been "spelled out" in lines.

4. If two letters side-by-side have the same numerological value (e, n = 5, 5), draw >< in the line where it crosses the box that contains that number.

5. Find the reduced sum of the letters in the complete keyword (39, which reduces to 3 by adding the digits: 3 + 9 = 12 then adding 1 + 2 = 3). Draw a small square in the line at that point. If you were using one of the larger magick squares, which include more numbered boxes, you'd put the small square in box 39.

6. Draw another small circle at the end of the line. This completes your sigil, the magickal symbol or glyph for "strength."

7. If you wish, draw appropriate astrological symbols, your birthchart, or the signs and degrees of your sun, moon, planets, Part of Fortune, nodes, and angles on the reverse side of the paper sigil. You can also include pictures of things that represent your intent, symbols from the tarot or runes, hexagrams from the *I Ching*, or whatever images signify strength for you.

4	9	2
3	5	7
8	1	6

Saturn

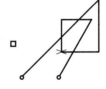

(Figure 10.5)

Magickal Alphabets

Instead of using numbers in the square, you could use letters from one of the magickal alphabets. Hebrew, Coptic, Ogham, runes, Enochian, Greek, Egyptian hieroglyphs, and Sanskrit are some alphabets used for magickal purposes. Choose the one that you feel most comfortable with or one that is associated with your own heritage. Hebrew, the language of the Kabbalah, is probably the most commonly used magickal alphabet, but I've never felt any kinship with Hebrew letters and prefer to use English or Ogham instead because I am of Celtic descent.

Other Tips for Creating Sigils

As with any type of magickal work, your intention is the most important factor when drawing a sigil. Here are a few additional suggestions you may want to use.

→ Create your sigil on a day that relates to your intent. For instance, a sigil for strength is best fashioned on Saturday, which corresponds to Saturn (see Chapter 9).

→ When drawing a sigil, check solar and lunar phases as well as planetary positions to make sure they are in harmony with your intention.

→ Draw it on paper or with ink of a color that's appropriate for your intent (for example, pink for love, green for money).

→ Dot the paper with oil or water that's scented with an astrologically appropriate botanical.

→ Some people say that when creating a sigil, you shouldn't let your shadow fall over the drawing.

Chapter 11

Spellworking

"A spell is a symbolic act done in an altered state of consciousness, in order to cause a desired change."

—Starhawk

Spellworking is one method magicians employ to shape and direct their lives. Generally, spells incorporate visualization, concentration, aligning yourself with cosmic and natural forces, and projecting your intention into the spiritual world as well as the manifest one. They may also include chanting or affirmations, ritual movements, and the use of various magickal tools or materials.

The most important part of any spell is your intention. Your thoughts, will, desire, and feeling are the power behind the spell—not the material ingredients that go into the formulation of a magickal mojo. A mojo is a magick charm to attract love, health, protection, prosperity, happiness, and so on, or to ward off harm.

Before you perform any type of magick, you need to put yourself in the right frame of mind. This means letting go of stress, negative emotions, and distractions due to ordinary, everyday concerns. To do your best magickal work, you want to be calm, balanced, alert, and clear-headed. Use whatever practice will enable you to reach this still, centered state: meditation, prayer, breathing techniques, yoga, or taking a soothing bath. Avoid drinking alcohol or using drugs before working magick, as these can alter your vital energy and interfere with your ability to focus your intent with clarity. (It is true that some magick involves ingesting mind-expanding substances, but this is usually done by knowledgeable magicians in specialized circumstances, not by beginners.)

Casting a Circle

The circle is a symbol of wholeness and it is often used to define sacred space. Its perimeter serves as a protective boundary between the outer world and the consecrated area within the circle. Magicians cast a circle around themselves when they work in order to keep out any unwanted energies that might interfere with their magick and to contain desired energies until the time is right to let them manifest.

A circle can be physically drawn on the floor or ground around the place where you are working, or you can create one with your imagination. It can be any size, as large or small as you need it to be. The simplest way to cast a circle is to envision yourself ringed by pure, white light. You can do this quickly, easily, at any time or place when you feel a need to protect yourself. You can also surround someone or something else with a circle of protective light. I often do this to shield my cats from harm.

Because magickal work depends heavily on the magician's ability to focus and direct intention, some people prefer to use more dramatic or active rituals for circle-casting. Generally, the more power and clarity you invest in your magick, the more effective it will be, so if performing a ceremony of some type helps you to get into the spirit of things and channel your mental energy better, by all means do it. Below is a basic ritual for casting a magickal circle. If you prefer, design your own ritual employing words and practices that are appropriate to your needs, your belief system, and your purposes. Or, refer to another book on magick for suggestions.

Before casting a circle, clear the area physically and/or with your imagination. Some people burn sage to purify sacred space. You might want to sweep the air with a broom or wave your arms across the area to brush away any unwanted energies. Or, you can simply envision the space being filled with pure white light.

1. Relax and calm your mind, using whichever method you prefer.

2. Move to the East section of your room or the area where you'll be working. If you have an athame or magick wand, draw the circle with it. Otherwise, just use your finger.

3. Extend your arm, pointing your athame or wand toward the East, and draw an invoking pentagram in the air before you (see figure 11.1). As you do this, visualize the shape taking form as blue-white light and say, "Guardians of the East, angels of Air, please guide and protect me. Lend your power and blessing to this spell, if it be your will."

Start

Invoking Pentagram

(Figure 11.1)

4. Walk in a clockwise direction to the South corner of your room, using your athame or wand to draw an arc of blue-white light around the area where you will be working.

5. Extend your arm, pointing your athame or wand toward the South. As you draw another pentagram of blue-white light in the air before you, say, "Guardians of the South, angels of Fire, please guide and protect me. Lend your power and blessing to this spell, if it be your will."

6. Continue walking clockwise, drawing an arc of blue-white light around your sacred space, until you reach the West.

7. Draw another pentagram of blue-white light in the air before you and say, "Guardians of the West, angels of Water, please guide and protect me. Lend your power and blessing to this spell, if it be your will."

8. Continue walking clockwise, drawing an arc of blue-white light around your sacred space, until you reach the North.

9. Draw a final pentagram of blue-white light in the air before you and say, "Guardians of the North, angels of Earth, please guide and protect me. Lend your power and blessing to this spell, if it be your will."

10. Continue walking clockwise, drawing an arc of blue-white light around your sacred space, until you return to the East, where you began. This completes the circle. Now say, "This space is protected by Divine white light. It is cleared of all harmful, disruptive, and unbalanced energies and filled with healing, harmonious energies. All work performed within this sacred space is done in accord with Divine Will and for the good of all concerned."

If you wish, you can incorporate the four elements into your circle-casting. You'll need a bowl of water, a bowl of sand or salt, and a stick of incense or bundle of sage for this part of the ritual. Light the incense or sage. Beginning at the East, walk clockwise around the area you wish to consecrate, trailing the smoke behind you until you have completed the circle. As you walk, say "With fire and air I cast this circle." Beginning at the East again, walk clockwise around the space once more, sprinkling water as you go. While you walk, say "With water I cast this circle." Repeat this procedure, sprinkling sand or salt, and say "With earth I cast this circle."

You may now enact your magickal work within the circle you've cast, knowing that you are safe and protected. If at any time you must leave the circle, cut a "door" in it with your athame, wand, or finger, starting at the floor. Step through the opening and close it after you by drawing the door again in reverse. Repeat these actions when you re-enter the circle.

When you've completed your magick, open the circle. Begin at the East and walk counterclockwise, tracing the circle backwards with your athame, wand, or hand. At each compass point, stop and thank the deities who have assisted you. Finally, move to the northwest. Point your athame, wand, or hand at the floor/ground and hold the other arm straight up over your head as you declare, "This circle is open, but unbroken. Let the magick created herein flow out and manifest in the world, in harmony with Divine Will and for the good of all concerned. Let all entities attracted to this spell (or ritual) return home, doing harm to none, and let there be peace between us. So be it now."

Take a few moments to ground the energies you've raised and to return to your normal state of consciousness. Envision or sense the power you've tapped flowing down through your body, to your feet, and into the earth below. Some magicians actually touch the ground to "earth the power."

Get Your Mojo Working

The spells below blend the astrological properties of natural objects—stones, botanicals, metals, fabrics, and so on—into talismans, in order to tap the energies of the cosmos and nature for human purposes. It's best to perform these spells during the appropriate lunar, solar, and hourly cycles as outlined in Chapter 9.

Charging Talismans and Amulets

To enhance the power of your magickal mojo, you can "charge" it with the four elements. When you've finished creating your talisman or amulet, pass it through the smoke from a candle flame or burning incense and say "I charge you with fire and air." (The color of the candle or the ingredients in the incense should correspond to the nature of the spell you are working.) Next, sprinkle your mojo with water and say "I charge you with water." Then sprinkle it with salt and say "I charge you with earth."

Remember, magickal mojos are not toys. They should never be used to harm or manipulate other people, to force them to act against their will, or even to help them unless you've obtained their permission beforehand. A word to the wise: Be careful what you ask for!

Herbal Protection Spell

We all need a little extra protection from time to time. Here's an herbal mojo you can make to help keep you or someone else safe. If possible, do this enchantment during the full moon, on Thursday, on the seventh hour of the day.

1. Collect nine from the following list of botanicals: fennel, blessed thistle, verbena, St. John's wort, alfalfa, star anise, ash bark or leaf, basil, peony seeds, snapdragon petals, thyme, chamomile flowers, pussy willow. You only need a small amount.

2. Gather together the following items: a circular piece of cloth or pouch of blue silk, a silver coin or piece of silver jewelry (ideally it should be circular or in the shape of a crescent moon), a small quartz crystal, and a small piece of jade, amber, or turquoise (you can use all three if you wish).

3. Relax, put your mind at ease, and focus all your attention on the project before you.

4. Create a special space in which to make your mojo by casting a circle according to the directions above.

5. Place all the objects you've collected in the circle of blue silk and tie it with a piece of white silk cord or thread. Make nine knots in the cord, and as you tie each one, speak or think: "This amulet protects the bearer at all times and in all situations."

6. Charge the mojo.

7. When you have finished, open the circle and thank the deities who have assisted you in your spellworking.

8. Carry your magickal mojo in your pocket during the day and place it under your pillow at night to protect you.

Love Charm

Since ancient times, people have used magickal charms or mojos to improve their love lives. Love charms often incorporate botanicals, gemstones, colors, and sigils that have special meaning for the person involved. If your intent is to attract a lover, the best time to prepare your love charm is between the new and the full moon, on Friday, and/or when the moon is in Libra.

1. Collect six from the following list of herbs. Use flowers, leaves, roots, or seeds. You don't need a lot, a pinch will do: lavender, red or pink rose petals (red symbolizes passion, pink is linked with romance), celery seed, cocoa, columbine, myrtle, raspberry, jasmine, daisy, and blackberry.

2. Gather together the following items: a pouch or circular piece of rose-colored silk cloth, a copper coin or piece of

copper jewelry in the shape of a circle, and a small piece of rose quartz and/or diamond.

3. Relax, put your mind at ease, and focus all your attention on the project before you.

4. Create a special space in which to make your mojo by casting a circle according to the directions above.

5. Place all the objects you've collected in the circle or pouch of silk and tie it with a piece of red silk cord or thread. Make six knots in the cord, and as you tie each one, say or think: "This talisman brings me the love that is right for me, in harmony with Divine Will, our own true wills, and with good to all concerned." (Feel free to create your own affirmation if you wish.)

6. Charge the mojo.

7. When you've finished, open the circle and thank the deities who have assisted you in your spellworking.

8. Carry your mojo in your pocket during the day and place it under your pillow at night to attract your soul mate. If you know feng shui, put it in the relationship gua of your home.

Prosperity Spell

Many people block their ability to receive abundance and prosperity because they believe that wealth isn't compatible with spirituality. We need to remember that money isn't evil—selling your soul to get it is. Using magick to attract prosperity is simply a way of tapping the infinite abundance that exists in the universe—you aren't depriving anyone else of his/her share. The best time to do this spell is during the waxing moon, on Thursday or Friday, and/or when the moon is in Taurus.

1. Collect eight from the following list: peppermint, cinnamon, hollyhock, cumin, catnip, rice, cedar, spearmint, clover (especially a four-leaf one), dandelion, cloves, cocoa. You only need a small amount.

2. Gather together the following items: a circular piece of cloth or pouch of green or gold silk, a coin (a silver dollar is best), a small piece of tiger eye and a small piece of aventurine. You can include a pentagram (or a drawing of one on a piece of parchment) if you wish. If you make plenty of money, but have trouble holding on to it, add a piece of hematite.

3. Relax, put your mind at ease, and focus all your attention on the project before you.

4. Create a special space in which to make your mojo by casting a circle.

5. Place all the objects you've collected in the pouch or circle of silk and tie it with a piece of gold or silver cord, ribbon, or thread. Make eight knots in the cord, and as you tie each one, speak or think: "This talisman attracts to me riches and abundance of all kinds, in harmony with Divine Will and with good to all concerned."

6. Charge your mojo.

7. When you have finished, open the circle and thank the deities who have assisted you in your spellworking.

8. Carry your magickal mojo in your pocket during the day and place it under your pillow at night to increase your prosperity. If you know feng shui, put it in the wealth gua of your home.

Lucky Ribbon Talisman

Create this talisman to attract three things you desire. For example, you may want to draw money, love, and good health into your life. Or, you might wish to move to a new home in a good neighborhood, get your book published, and meet interesting new friends. Your wishes can be general or specific, grand or simple.

Do this spell during the waxing moon, preferably between the Winter Solstice and the Summer Solstice. If all three of your desires share a planetary ruler (for example, Venus is linked with love, money, and creativity), perform the spell on the day and hour associated with that planet.

After casting a circle:

1. Relax, put your mind at ease, and focus all your attention on the project before you.

2. Cut three pieces of ribbon, each about 18 inches long. Each ribbon should be of a color that corresponds to your wish, for example, pink for love, green for money or health, blue for peace of mind, or purple for wisdom.

3. Write one wish or affirmation on each piece of ribbon. State your desire clearly, positively, and in the present tense. For instance, write "I now have a wonderful job that gives me everything I want and need and I am very happy." Doing this convinces your subconscious to manifest the condition you desire ASAP, rather than at some time in the future. State exactly what you want, without ambiguity, and make sure you don't overlook anything. For instance, if you say "I am now in love with a wonderful man and he is in love with me" you might end up attracting a wonderful man who happens to be married to someone else! If you don't know exactly what you want, leave the details up to Divine Will by including the phrase "this is perfect for me in every way."

4. After you have written a wish on each ribbon, braid the three pieces together. Repeat your three wishes aloud as you work and envision them coming true.

5. Charge your ribbon talisman.

6. When you have finished, open the circle and thank the deities who have assisted you in your spellworking.

7. Wear the finished braid or place it in a spot where you'll see it often, so that it reminds you of your intentions each time you look at it.

Invisibility Spell

This protection spell veils you in secrecy and keeps you from attracting the attention of people whom you don't want to see you, so you can go about your business in private. Don't worry, you won't actually disappear! The best time to perform this spell is during the early morning of the Summer Solstice. You can also do it on the new moon in Scorpio or Pisces.

1. Pick a fern leaf or gather fern seeds just before the stroke of midnight on the Summer Solstice.

2. Gather together the following items: a circular piece of cloth or a pouch of black silk, a small piece of sardonyx, and some heliotrope oil. If you also feel a need to protect yourself from harm, add a piece of amber and/or a small bloodstone.

3. Relax, put your mind at ease, and focus all your attention on the project before you.

4. Create a special space in which to make your mojo by casting a circle according to the directions above.

5. Place all the objects you've collected in the pouch or circle of silk and tie it with a piece of black cord, ribbon, or thread. Make seven knots in the cord, and as you tie each

one, speak or think: "This amulet prevents me from being seen by anyone who shouldn't see me and keeps me safe at all times."

6. Imagine that you are completely surrounded by a protective fog or veil that shields you from prying eyes.

7. Charge your mojo.

8. When you have finished, open the circle and thank the deities who have assisted you in your spellworking.

9. Carry your magickal mojo in your pocket when you want to remain unseen.

Moon Magick

Each month the moon offers new opportunities to manifest your dreams. Lunar phases energize your spells and help them work more effectively, so pay attention to this heavenly body's position when you do magick. The waxing moon encourages growth, the waning moon favors decrease.

New Moon Abundance Ritual

Perform this ritual just as the new moon begins to wax. After casting a circle:

1. Relax, put your mind at ease, and focus all your attention on the project before you.

2. On a large sheet of paper or cardboard (artist's mat board is best), list up to 10 wishes you want to come true. You can ask for health, prosperity, love, friendship, a new job —whatever you desire. Remember, you aren't depriving anyone else by asking for what you want—you are merely tapping into the infinite abundance that is always present in the universe. Use ink or crayon colors that correspond to your wishes (green for money, red or pink

for love, and so on). Be sure these wishes do not harm anyone else, though, and if they involve another person, ask that individual's permission before making a wish that will affect him or her.

3. Your subconscious responds to images better than words, so enhance your list by drawing or pasting pictures from magazines that illustrate your wishes—the new car or house you want, for example. I did this spell once to get a new computer and the company I worked for soon bought me exactly the model I'd wished for.

4. Don't specify exactly how your wishes will manifest. A friend of mine needed money and initially asked that it come to her as a result of her own efforts. I explained that she was limiting her options and she eliminated the stipulation. Soon she received a letter from her mortgage company advising her of an error in her favor; a rebate check was enclosed.

5. When you've finished, light a candle and set it in a candlestick at the center of your illustrated list. Choose a candle of a color that corresponds to your wishes. If your wishes run the gamut, burn a multicolored candle or a black one (black contains all colors).

6. Read your list aloud and ask your spirit guides to grant your wishes. I recommend adding a qualifying statement such as, "This is accomplished now, in harmony with Divine Will, my own true will, and for the good of all concerned."

7. Let the candle burn down completely. Thank your guides for their assistance, then open your circle.

8. Give your spell a chance to work—complicated wishes may require some time. Be confident that your wishes will come true in the proper time and manner.

Waxing Moon Knot Spell

You'll need a piece of string or cord the length of your body for this spell. Perform it during the moon's waxing period, preferably no later than halfway between the new and full moons. After casting a circle:

1. Relax, put your mind at ease, and focus all your attention on the project before you.

2. Make a wish for something you want to manifest in your life—love, money, success, happiness, and so on. As you think or speak your wish, tie a knot in the cord. Envision the wish coming true.

3. Make a second wish. Tie another knot.

4. Make as many wishes as you like, tying each into the cord.

5. When you've finished, thank your spirit guides for bringing your wishes to fruition. Open the circle.

6. You can wear your cord or hang it in a place where you will see it often. When all the wishes have come true, remove the cord and burn it in a ritual fire, giving thanks to the deities who have helped manifest your wishes.

Waning Moon Bond-Breaking Ritual

Perform this ritual during the moon's waning period, preferably three days before the new moon, to break an unwanted bond between yourself and another person. After casting a circle:

1. Relax, put your mind at ease.

2. Sit quietly inside the circle with your eyes closed.

3. Call the person you want to release into your imagination and ask him/her to sit in a small circle just outside the circle you've cast to protect yourself.

4. As you gaze at this person, you'll notice some type of connecting material flowing between his/her solar plexus and yours—it may resemble a heavy cord, a steel bar, a band of light, a chain. This represents the bond between you—pay attention to its substance and how the connection feels.

5. Imagine yourself cutting this bond in two, using whatever tool you need for the job: scissors, a knife, a chainsaw, a blowtorch. You may actually experience a slight twinge of pain or a sudden jolt when you do this. Mentally tie off the two ends of the connection, as if you were tying a newborn baby's umbilical cord (tie your own first, then the other person's). Now visualize soothing blue-green light healing your solar plexus and the other person's.

6. Release this person from your life with the words:

    > "I respect your path and set you free.
    > Fare thee well and blessed be."

7. Allow the other person's image to fade away, then open your eyes. When you are ready, open the circle.

8. Depending on the strength of the bond between you, it may be necessary to repeat this ritual several times until you've severed the connection completely.

Magickal Mandalas

Mandalas are elaborate and very powerful circular images that symbolize the world. The word mandala means circle in Sanskrit. Although they are usually painted or drawn, mandalas can be fabricated in virtually any media—even danced—and frequently contain archetypal, spiritual, or magickal symbolism. Alchemically, they often represent the synthesis of the four elements and thus signify union and harmony. In Tibetan Buddhism, these patterns are used to aid meditation. C. G. Jung understood the therapeutic potential of mandalas and used them extensively in his spiritual psychology work. According to Jung, "the mandala is the centre. It is the exponent of all paths. It is the path to the centre, the path to individuation."

Wonderful mandalas can be found in ancient mosques, temples, and churches, in domed ceilings and inlaid mosaic floor patterns, as well as in religious and occult texts. The rose windows in Europe's great cathedrals are beautiful examples of mandalas. So are some oriental carpets. Horoscope wheels and the bagua used in feng shui are also mandalas. We even find mandalas in nature—lotus flowers and daisies, sea urchin shells and sand dollars are naturally occurring mandalas.

You can design a magickal mandala of your own and incorporate universal and personal imagery into it, according to your specific purposes. As you create your mandala, you imbue it with intention so that it becomes an embodiment of your vision, feelings, and objectives. Once finished, the mandala continues to reflect the magickal energy you've focused on it back to you—each time you look at it, you are reminded consciously and subconsciously of your intention.

As you begin designing your mandala, you may wish to keep the image of the world or the universe in mind. The upper portion of the circle might represent the sky, the lower part the earth. Or, the upper half could symbolize the conscious mind and the outer world, the lower half the inner, subconscious dimension. The left side of the circle could signify yourself, the right side might describe your relationships with other people—just as the hemispheres of the birthchart do.

I frequently incorporate tarot or astrological symbolism into my mandalas. Sometimes I include spirit animals, birds, reptiles, and mythological creatures; other times I paint mandalas with nature scenes that depict the four elements. Numbers, *I Ching* hexagrams, sigils, alchemical symbols, letters or words from your native language or another alphabet (runes, Ogham, Arabic, Chinese, Hebrew, and so on) can also be used effectively in your design. You might want to select colors that convey your purposes, too.

For example, if your intent in creating a mandala is to attract love, consider using pink and red as your predominant colors. Incorporate the astrological glyphs for Venus and Libra, perhaps Mars (sexuality/passion) and the moon (home/family/emotions), into your pattern. The numbers two and six are associated with give and take, shared experiences, and harmony, so they could be beneficial to include. In the tarot, cups represent emotions and are usually connected with relationships. Roses and gardenias, because of their link to the zodiac sign Libra, might also enhance your mandala's beauty and purpose. There is no right or wrong way to design a mandala—choose whatever images speak to you.

As you create your mandala, focus on your intention and project this into your work. Remember, you aren't just painting a pretty picture—although it may turn out to be quite beautiful—the entire process is a magick act. Whatever thoughts and feelings you put into your mandala will be mirrored back to you each time you view the finished product.

Place the completed mandala in a spot where you'll see it often, so that its meaning continues to impress itself on your subconscious. If you know something about feng shui, you may wish to hang it in the appropriate sector or gua of your home or office, thereby combining the power of two different magickal systems.

Chapter 12

Astrology As a Predictive Tool

"We are part of a higher spiritual context, which determines our qualities and our destiny."

—Rudolf Steiner

Throughout recorded history—perhaps since the beginning of time—human beings have sought to divine the future, to preview our destinies by interpreting mysterious patterns in stones, yarrow stalks, dreams, visions, cards, clouds, fire, and planetary movements. We aren't content to simply let our lives unfold as they will; we want to prepare ourselves for what's coming and control the future as best we can.

Whether or not we are masters of our fate is the subject of much debate. I believe we participate in creating the circumstances in our lives, that "destiny" is a combination of free will and karma. I also believe that if we know what forces are operating at any given time, and what opportunities and obstacles lie ahead, we can make better choices.

Everyone possesses some ability to see into the future. We all experience hunches, such as thinking about someone just before he or she telephones, even though we usually don't pay much attention to them. Many people have precognitive dreams in which forthcoming events are revealed to them. Shortly before my father was killed in an automobile accident, for example, my siblings and I dreamt of his death.

Astrology has only recently developed as a guide to understanding personality. Historically, it was used to predict the future. The ancient Egyptians gazed into the heavens to determine when the Nile would overflow. Roman emperors frequently had their birthcharts cast to see whether their reigns would be successful. According to the Christmas story, the three wise men foresaw the birth of Jesus in the stars.

Today astrologers chart celestial movements to predict weather patterns, earthquakes, stock market trends, the outcomes of sporting events, and the elections of presidents, as well as the futures of ordinary individuals. When it comes to accurately timing situations, astrology is superior to most other methods. Tarot cards, runes, and the *I Ching* can only look ahead a few months, but planetary influences can be calculated into the next millennium.

Astrologers use a variety of techniques to predict future events and circumstances. Each technique involves different parameters, has different applications, and provides different insights. A solar return chart, which is calculated annually for the time when the sun reaches the exact position it occupied at the time of your birth, shows what issues will be important in your life during the coming year. Progressions describe how and when slowly developing situations will evolve. Horary charts answer a specific question, such as "Where is the cat?" and offer related information about when the cat might be found. Transits show how the positions of the planets in the sky at any given time influence a birthchart (or the chart of a country, business, event, relationship, and so on).

Planetary Transits

As the planets move through the heavens, they affect us in myriad ways, which is why our lives are not static. I find planetary transits to be the most revealing and dramatic indicators of what's to come, which is why I've chosen to discuss them, rather than the other astrological predictive methods, in this chapter. (I use the other methods, too, but can't possibly cover all of them here.) For a more comprehensive guide to these important celestial cycles, see Robert Hand's *Planets in Transit.*

Planetary transits provide temporary energetic focuses that can be either assets or liabilities when working magick. To take advantage of these energies, do magick that relates both to the transiting planet and to the house through which it is traveling at a particular time. Also consider the aspects a transiting planet makes to natal planets, as these can enhance or interfere with your success. Sextiles and trines from a transiting planet to a natal body are generally beneficial; conjunctions from the transiting sun, Venus, or Jupiter are favorable. Squares, inconjunctions, and oppositions between planets can limit the effectiveness of your spells, cause tension and upsets, or produce other difficulties, especially when the outer planets are involved.

To get an idea of what to expect during a particular transit, consider the nature of a transiting planet in connection with the areas of life represented by the house through which it is traveling. (You may want to refer to Chapter 3 if you are not already familiar with the meanings of the planets, houses, and aspects.) If Mars is currently moving through your seventh house, for instance, you know that lots of energy, action, and perhaps stress (Mars) will be focused on a primary relationship (seventh house). Then evaluate the impact of the transiting planet on any natal planet(s) it aspects. If transiting Mars is favorably aspecting natal Mercury, it will stimulate your mind.

This simplified process will not give you the complete picture—for that you need to synthesize all the factors in the entire chart—but it's a start. Astrological prediction is an art that requires many years of study, observation, and practice to perfect. Even so, the best of us misjudge situations or interpret information incorrectly at times.

Sun Transits

The sun remains in each house for approximately one month (depending on the size of the house) and takes a year to complete its passage through the entire chart. Because the sun's transits are regular, you can easily predict which house this luminary will occupy at any time during the year. For example, if your ascendant (the cusp of the first house) is 0 degrees of Capricorn, the sun will enter your first house every year on about December 21.

The sun's salubrious energy enhances whatever it shines upon in the birthchart. Its transits bring benefits of all kinds—vitality, self-confidence, opportunities, recognition, clarity. When the sun moves through a house, it focuses positive energy into the areas of life associated with that house. Affairs connected with a house generally improve under the sun's influence. For example, when the sun moves through your tenth house of career and public image, you may get a promotion, start a new job, or receive some type of success/notoriety.

When the sun makes a harmonious aspect to a natal planet, it brings out the best qualities of that planet, enabling you to utilize the planet's energy in a favorable way. The sun's nature is so beneficial that even the stressful aspects rarely cause problems. A sun transit to Mars, for instance, boosts your vitality, self-confidence, and sex appeal. It may also prompt fortunate experiences with men (for both men and women).

In magickal work

Do prosperity spells while the sun is in the second house, love spells when it's transiting the fifth or seventh. The sun in the ninth favors spiritual or physical journeys; in the 10th it increases the possibility of career success or fame. Harmonious sun-moon aspects are good for blessing your home or to improve a relationship with a spouse, child, or parent. Sun-Venus aspects are perfect for working magick to attract love and/or money. During sun-Jupiter aspects, do spells to ensure a safe and enjoyable trip, to gain recognition or success, or for general good luck. Sun-Saturn transits can help you overcome setbacks and obstacles, bless a business venture, or ease difficulties in a work situation.

Moon Transits

The moon moves very quickly, traveling through the entire chart every 28 days and remaining in a house for approximately two to three days (depending on the size of the house). Transiting aspects to a planet last only about a day.

The moon's passage through a house in the birthchart sensitizes you to issues associated with that house and might prompt related insights. During the period when the transiting moon occupies a particular house, your attention may be drawn to matters connected with that house. For example, feelings toward a spouse might be stimulated by the moon's transit of your seventh house; money issues may concern you while the moon is in your second house.

A lunar aspect to a planet triggers that planet's energy and sets off an emotional response. Stressful aspects may spark tension or oversensitivity; harmonious aspects can promote positive interactions, creativity, or feelings of affection. A beneficial aspect between the moon and Mercury, for instance, helps you blend intellect and intuition. A stressful aspect from the moon to Mars can make you impatient, impulsive, or argumentative.

In magickal work

Consider the moon's phase as well as its position in the birthchart—the waxing moon encourages growth, the waning moon favors decrease. New moons are good for beginnings, full moons bring matters to fruition.

Lunar transits can produce fluctuating circumstances and therefore may be advantageous or problematic when working magick, depending on your intention. For example, a lunar transit of the second house might destabilize your finances rather than augmenting them. Therefore, do prosperity magick only when the moon is waxing in your second house. Because the moon is associated with creativity, its passage though the fifth house is an excellent time to do fertility magick. The moon in the 12th house or favorably aspecting Neptune improves your psychic ability and is thus helpful to divination or dreamwork. Harmonious moon-Venus aspects can be beneficial for love spells or doing magick for women friends and relatives.

Mercury Transits

Mercury completes its passage through the birthchart in about a year. Due to its retrograde periods, which occur once every four months, it can remain in a house for a couple weeks or a couple months (depending on the size of the house); an aspect between transiting Mercury and a natal planet lasts about one to three weeks.

Mercury's energy is relatively gentle; some people hardly notice its influence. When Mercury moves through a house, you tend to think and talk about things related to the affairs of that house. For instance, when Mercury transits your third house, you might telephone a brother you haven't talked to lately or spend time socializing with neighbors. Mercury's movement through the ninth house might prompt you to read a book about philosophy or religion.

A similar thing happens when transiting Mercury connects with a natal planet. Matters related to the natal planet become subjects for thought, study, and conversation. When Mercury connects with Mars, for example, you may think and talk a lot about sex. Depending on the planet or angle involved, transiting Mercury's presence can be mildly stimulating, though the action it triggers will probably be short-lived. A Mercury-Venus contact might prompt you to jot down a few love poems, but won't provide enough motivation to write a romance novel.

In magickal work

Tap Mercury's energy to send messages to people or non-physical entities. When this planet transits the eleventh house, it can aid your efforts to reconnect with an old friend; when it's in your third it facilitates communication with neighbors or siblings; its passage through your twelfth house can put you in touch with your spirit guides. Affirmations fall into this planet's domain, and you can use them to advantage during Mercury transits. Do affirmations to attract money when Mercury travels through the second house or positively aspects Venus. Blessings to protect a home are effective when Mercury transits the fourth house or aspects your moon favorably. Study magick while Mercury is in your eighth house or aspecting Pluto.

Venus Transits

Venus circles the sun every 225 days, but because of retrograde periods it can take more than a year to complete its passage through the entire birthchart. Depending on when the retrograde cycle occurs and the size of the house, Venus usually remains in a house for about three weeks to three months. Aspects between transiting Venus and a natal planet can last about a week to a few months.

Venus rules love and money, and those are the two goodies you could receive during this planet's transits. Known as the "lesser benefic," Venus brings ease, abundance, and pleasant experiences wherever it goes. When this planet moves through a house, it focuses positive energy into that house and enhances related matters. For example, when Venus travels through the sixth house it promotes positive feelings toward work and coworkers. Venus can also help you attract—or spend—money in areas associated with the house it transits. When it moves though the second house, you could earn more money than usual; while it's in the fourth house you might spend a lot on home furnishings.

A contact from transiting Venus generally emphasizes the best qualities of a natal planet, although stressful aspects—particularly to Jupiter—can encourage laziness and indulgence. An aspect from Venus to Mars may prompt a passionate love affair; an aspect from Venus to Neptune stimulates imagination and might provide the impetus to paint, write, or compose music.

In magickal work

Do prosperity magick while Venus is in your second house, love spells when it transits the fifth or seventh house. When Venus is in your 10th, do magick to enhance your career or public image. Favorable aspects between transiting Venus and the moon, Venus and Venus, or Venus and Mars are also good for working love spells. Perform magick for success or good luck during Venus-Jupiter aspects. Venus aspects to Neptune can improve psychic receptivity and creativity.

Mars Transits

Mars takes about two years to travel through the birth-chart, remaining in a house for a couple months or several (depending on retrograde periods and the size of the house). During its direct motion, transiting aspects from Mars to a planet or angle last for a few weeks, although when Mars is retrograde they can stretch to a few months.

Mars' influence is stimulating and energizing and can be quite powerful. Whether you experience it as invigorating or stressful depends on the parts of the chart and the aspects involved. Mars transits are motivating factors and often spur action of some sort, especially if a matter has been pending for a while.

When Mars moves through a house in the birthchart, it focuses lots of restless energy and enthusiasm into areas connected with that house. A Mars transit of the second house, for instance, may inspire you to work extra hard to earn more money. When it travels through the fourth house, you might feel an urge to relocate. However, the agitating nature of this planet can also stir up tensions and disruption. A second-house transit could provoke disagreements about finances; arguments with family members might occur during a fourth-house transit.

Transiting Mars energizes the natal planets it aspects, as if giving them a shot of adrenaline. A sextile or trine from Mars to another heavenly body is usually experienced as favorable. An easy Mars-sun aspect heightens vitality; a Mars-Jupiter contact often indicates travel. Mars squares, inconjuncts, and oppositions produce stress and/or upsets. For example, a challenging aspect from transiting Mars to natal Venus may generate arguments with a lover. Mars-Saturn aspects might urge you to rebel against authority figures or responsibilities; Mars-Uranus can trigger accidents due to impatience or anger.

In magickal work

This planet's energy can be a bit tricky to work with because its stimulating nature may produce tension or conflict. Spells to increase physical strength or courage could be effective while Mars is in your first house. A Mars transit of the seventh house might boost a spell to rekindle passion in a marriage. Harmonious aspects from transiting Mars to the sun or Jupiter can aid spells to hasten career success or increase sexual vitality. Do magick to prompt action in stagnant conditions during sextiles or trines from transiting Mars to Saturn; do magick to overcome fears or obstacles when Mars aspects Pluto favorably.

Jupiter Transits

Jupiter completes its trip through the birthchart once every 12 years or so, remaining in each house for roughly a year (depending on retrograde periods and the size of the house). Aspects from transiting Jupiter to a natal planet or angle last approximately two months during periods of direct motion, but can stretch to about nine months during Jupiter's retrograde cycles.

Sometimes called the "greater benefic" by astrologers, Jupiter's influence is usually considered lucky and pleasant. This planet inspires optimism and expands whatever it touches. While this may be desirable in most cases, Jupiter's growth-producing nature knows no bounds and can produce excess or indulgence. This planet's movement though the 10th house often brings career success and recognition. Jupiter transits of the seventh house can mean luck in love; second-house transits improve your financial picture.

Harmonious aspects from transiting Jupiter (conjunction, sextile, or trine) highlight and expand a natal planet's qualities, enabling it to express itself more fully. When Jupiter connects with Mars, for instance, you experience increased vitality and self-confidence. Jupiter-moon aspects promote a sense of well-being and security; they can also enhance fertility and improve relationships with family members. Challenging Jupiter aspects (square, inconjunct, or opposition), on the other hand, can bring too much of a good thing. For example, Jupiter-Neptune contacts sometimes coincide with overuse of alcohol or drugs; Jupiter-Venus aspects can cause you to gain weight or blow your budget on luxuries.

In magickal work

The best time to do prosperity magick is when Jupiter moves through your second house. Love spells are strengthened by Jupiter transits through your fifth or seventh house. A Jupiter transit of your eighth house is a good time to do magick to get a loan or attract a financial backer. Positive aspects between transiting Jupiter and the sun are excellent for doing magick to land a job, gain recognition or fame, or increase your vitality. Jupiter-moon aspects promote fertility; Jupiter-Venus aspects are ideal for love spells; Jupiter-Saturn aspects can help spells to bless a business venture.

Saturn Transits

Saturn takes approximately 29 years to travel through the birthchart. It spends about two to four years in each house (depending on retrograde periods and the size of the house) and aspects a natal planet or angle for periods of about five months to a year (during retrogradation).

The planet of limitation and discipline, Saturn often brings responsibilities, tests, and difficult lessons during its transits. Hard work and pragmatism are required to produce the positive results associated with this planet. When Saturn moves through the sixth house, health problems—especially chronic conditions and ailments connected with work or an unhealthy lifestyle—may arise. A Saturn transit of the 12th house often requires you to let go of people and things that are inhibiting your personal development.

Stressful aspects from transiting Saturn to a natal planet restrict that planet's ability to express itself and cause you to take a hard look at issues related to that planet. Saturn-Venus aspects, for instance, may coincide with the end of an unfulfilling relationship or force you to budget your resources more carefully. Harmonious aspects from Saturn, however, can stabilize situations and bring well-deserved rewards. A Saturn-sun trine might result in a promotion you have earned; a Saturn-Neptune sextile could help an artist bring ideas down to earth and make money through creative efforts.

In magickal work

Saturn's influence can aid spells to bind an enemy or banish unwanted energies. Do magick to protect your home when Saturn transits the fourth house. Spells to break unwanted ties or end restrictive situations are strengthened while Saturn is in your 12th house. To move a romance toward marriage, do a love spell when transiting Saturn is favorably aspecting Venus. Spells for long-term business success can be augmented by an easy aspect from transiting Saturn to the sun or midheaven. Positive Saturn-Jupiter contacts aid spells to reduce spending and help you get out of debt.

Uranus Transits

Uranus takes 84 years to complete its trip through the birthchart, and it remains in a house for several years. An aspect from transiting Uranus to a natal planet can last a couple of years. Because Uranus and the other slow-moving outer planets influence you for such long periods, their impact on your life is usually quite dramatic.

Uranus is the planet of change; whatever it transits in your chart gets thoroughly shaken up. Generally, the changes you experience are unexpected, sudden, and powerful. It's almost impossible to predict exactly what the outcome will be—all that can be said with certainty is that things won't be the same afterward. When Uranus travels through a house, it creates disruption, excitement, and awakenings in areas related to that house. For instance, Uranus in the second house usually alters your finances, sometimes causing ups and downs for several years. Uranus in the seventh house can bring an abrupt end to a marriage or prompt a sudden, unconventional love relationship—or both.

Contacts from transiting Uranus stimulate and change circumstances connected with the planets it aspects. Often the effect is rather like getting hit by lightning, especially in the case of a conjunction, square, or opposition. If Uranus aspects your sun, your sense of yourself and your image may suddenly shift. Uranus transits to the moon alter your home life radically, sometimes through the birth of a child, relocation, or divorce. Because this planet is associated with independence, its transits often produce a newly found sense of freedom, although the process may be quite upsetting or difficult.

In magickal work

Working with Uranian energy can produce sudden, unexpected results, so magick that utilizes it is hard to control or direct. If you do a love spell while Uranus is in the seventh house, for example, you may attract an exciting and unusual relationship or bring an abrupt end to an existing marriage. A good time to study magick or astrology is when Uranus moves through the ninth house. Do magick to eliminate barriers, change the status quo, or break up static conditions during a positive aspect between transiting Uranus and natal Saturn. Spells to stimulate ideas and inventiveness can benefit from Uranus-Mercury aspects. If you want to change your image, do magick when Uranus makes a favorable aspect to the sun or your ascendant.

Neptune Transits

It takes 165 years for Neptune to cycle through the birthchart, so it influences a house or natal planet for quite a few years. Neptune's job is to dissolve physical limitations and forms, and that's exactly what it does during its transits. In the process, it creates lots of confusion, illusions, and fantasies.

When Neptune travels through a house in your chart, it casts a fog over matters associated with that house, making it hard to see things clearly. Escapism, idealism, spiritual inclinations, deception, and heightened sensitivity often accompany this planet's transits. Neptune's passage through the fifth house may bring increased creativity and/or a highly romantic (and perhaps unrealistic) love affair. When this planet moves through your 10th house, your career goals can become confused, professional relationships might dissolve, or your public image may be tarnished by scandal or deception.

The same sensitivity and lack of clarity coincide with Neptune's transiting aspects to natal planets, causing matters associated with the affected planet to grow muddy or slip away entirely, especially if the aspect is a challenging one. A contact between transiting Neptune and natal Mars, for example, may sap your vitality. Neptune acting on Saturn dissolves boundaries, security, and structures. When Neptune transits Venus, all sorts of confusion and unrealistic expectations surround relationships.

In magickal work

Intuitive and creative abilities are enhanced during Neptune transits. While this planet increases psychic sensitivity, it also interferes with clarity; therefore, working with its energy can produce unforeseen results or effects. For example, a love spell done while Neptune is in your fifth house or aspecting Venus may attract a partner who is very romantic but completely unreliable. Although Neptune in the ninth house or aspecting Mercury can aid spiritual development, you might have difficulty determining which teacher is right for you. This slow-moving planet remains in a house for many years, so its influence in matters pertaining to the affairs of a house may not be as important in magickal work as its aspects to planets in your birthchart.

Pluto Transits

The outermost planet in our solar system, Pluto takes about 248 years to complete its journey through the birthchart. Due to its highly irregular cycle, this planet may remain in a house for a decade or for more than 30 years, and it can aspect a planet in the natal chart for many years. Of all the planets, Pluto is probably the most difficult to handle and its effects are the most profound.

Sometimes called the destroyer, Pluto is linked with death and rebirth. As it moves through the chart, it systematically tears down and eliminates whatever it touches in order to make room for new growth. Astrologers like to use the word "transformation" in connection with Pluto, which, although accurate, does not convey the painful and frightening nature of what happens during this planet's transits. (In *The Astrology of Fate,* Liz Greene offers valuable insights about Pluto.)

When Pluto moves through a house in the birthchart, it dredges up hidden issues connected with that house and forces you to confront them. Anything that is no longer useful is ruthlessly destroyed—although sometimes you don't realize what's transpired until after Pluto's transit is over and the dust settles. Pluto's passage through the fourth house awakens family problems and childhood traumas, undermining your sense of security and your ability to control your home life. When Pluto transits your ninth house, your spiritual or philosophical views may be radically altered, or you might relocate to a distant part of the world.

Transiting Pluto also transforms matters related to the natal planets it aspects. A Pluto-Mercury aspect will dramatically change your way of thinking and communicating. Pluto-Venus transits often destroy relationships, but they also prompt powerful, seemingly fated romances. When Pluto connects with your sun, you may deeply question yourself and your purpose in life, ultimately remaking yourself after coming face to face with your dark side.

In magickal work

Pluto transits are potentially advantageous for most magickal work, however, stressful aspects between transiting Pluto and natal planets are often too intense and destructive to utilize effectively. Positive contacts between Pluto and Venus can aid prosperity magick, especially when another person's resources are involved. This energy can also be very powerful in love spells or sex magick. Easy aspects between Pluto and the sun can strengthen spells for professional success or personal transformation.

Pluto transits can also be advantageous when doing magick to break bonds, overcome obstacles, or increase your power against an enemy. This slow-moving planet remains in a house for many years, so its influence in matters pertaining to the affairs of a house may not be as important in magickal work as its aspects to planets in your birthchart.

Astrology and the Body

Sun/Leo/5th house:
Heart, back, spinal cord.

Moon/Cancer/4th house:
Breasts, stomach, uterus.

Mercury/Gemini/3rd house:
Hands, arms, shoulders, lungs, nervous system.

Mercury/Virgo/6th house:
Nervous system, digestive system, pancreas, gall bladder.

Venus/Taurus/2nd house:
Neck/throat, thyroid gland, mouth.

Venus/Libra/7th house:
Kidneys, bladder, veins.

Mars/Aries/1st house:
Head/face, eyes, muscles, adrenal glands.

Jupiter/Sagittarius/9th house:
Liver, thighs, blood, hips.

Saturn/Capricorn/10th house:
Bones, teeth, skin, knees, nails, hair.

Uranus/Aquarius/11th house:
Calves, ankles, circulatory system, pituitary gland.

Neptune/Pisces/12th house:
Feet, lymph system, pineal gland.

Pluto/Scorpio/8th house:
Sex organs, elimination system.

Max Heindel's Musical/Astrological Correspondences

Sound healers often work with these tonal frequencies (which also correspond to the seven major chakras) to produce harmony within the body.

Sun/Leo:	A
Moon/Cancer:	G♯
Mercury/Gemini:	F♯
Mercury/Virgo:	C♯
Venus/Taurus:	E
Venus/Libra:	D♭
Mars/Aries:	D
Jupiter/Sagittarius:	F♭
Saturn/Capricorn:	G
Uranus/Aquarius:	A
Neptune/Pisces:	B
Pluto/Scorpio:	E

Hebrew Letters and Their Astrological Correspondences

Bet:	Mercury
Daled:	Venus
Gimel:	Moon
Kaf:	Jupiter
Pey:	Mars
Resh:	Sun
Taf:	Saturn
Ayin:	Capricorn
Khet:	Cancer
Hey:	Aries
Lamed:	Libra
Nun:	Scorpio
Koof:	Pisces
Samekh:	Sagittarius
Tet:	Leo
Tzaddi:	Aquarius
Vav:	Taurus
Yud:	Virgo
Zayin:	Gemini

Druid Alphabet and Day of the Week Astrological Correspondences

Consonants:

Aries:	S	Libra:	G
Taurus:	H	Scorpio:	P (NG)
Gemini:	D, T	Sagittarius:	B, R
Cancer:	C	Capricorn:	L
Leo:	Q	Aquarius:	N
Virgo:	M	Pisces:	F (V)

Vowels:

Sun/Venus:	U	Jupiter:	E
Moon:	A	Saturn:	I
Mercury:	O		

Days of the Week:

Sunday:	Sun	Thursday:	Jupiter
Monday:	Moon	Friday:	Venus
Tuesday:	Mars	Saturday:	Saturn
Wednesday:	Mercury		

Greek Letters and Their Astrological Correspondences

Sun: Rho

Moon: Upsilon

Mercury: Beta

Venus: Delta

Mars: Pi

Jupiter: Kappa

Saturn: Tau

Arabic Letters and Their Astrological Correspondences

Aries: A, H

Taurus: ', Gh

Gemini: Kh, Q

Cancer: K, J

Leo: Sh, Y

Virgo: L, N

Libra: R

Scorpio: D, T

Sagittarius: S

Capricorn: Z, Th

Aquarius: Dh, F, B

Pisces: M, W

Meditation for Balancing Chakras

1. Sit comfortably, keeping your back straight, and relax using whatever method you prefer.

2. Visualize a ball of deep red light glowing at the base of your spine (the root chakra). In the center of this ball of light, envision the symbol for Saturn. You may experience a tingling sensation, a pleasant warmth, an enhanced sense of security, a feeling of power, or other impressions. Hold this image in your mind for a few minutes or as long as you wish.

3. Imagine the energy moving up to about a hand's width below your belly button. Envision orange light glowing here as you superimpose the symbols for Mars and Pluto on this chakra.

4. After a few minutes, feel the energy moving upward as you focus your attention on your solar plexus (a few inches above your belly button). Imagine a ball of yellow light here, together with the symbols for the moon and Jupiter.

5. Now, let the energy rise into the area of your heart and visualize brilliant green light glowing here. This may awaken feelings of love and compassion. In your mind's eye, see the symbol for the sun in the center of the ball of green light.

6. Feel the energy flow upward to the base of your throat. Imagine blue light and the symbols for Venus and Mercury in this area.

7. Move the energy to the region of the "third eye" between your eyebrows. Visualize the symbol for Uranus superimposed on a circle of indigo light.

8. Allow the energy to rise to the top of your head. Envision purple light glowing like a halo around your head and see the symbol for Neptune in the center of it.

By the end of this meditation, you should experience a sense of increased relaxation and serenity. Feelings of tension, tightness, or discomfort in any of the chakras may indicate blockages in these areas. Over time, this meditation can help open up the energy centers so they function more effectively.

Glossary

Affirmation: A positive statement designed to create a change.

Alchemy: The process of magickally transforming one substance into another.

Air: One of the four elements. It is associated with mental activity and communication.

Amulet: A magick charm to protect against unwanted energies.

Angles: Angles are sensitive points in a horoscope. The term is generally used in connection with the most important angles—the ascendant, descendant, midheaven, and imum colei—which partition an astrological chart into quadrants.

Ascendant: An important angle in an astrological chart. The degree of the zodiac that was rising on the eastern horizon at the moment and the place of birth; the beginning of the first house in an astrological chart.

Aspect: An angular relationship that produces an energetic connection between two or more celestial bodies or points in an astrological chart so that they influence each other. The most significant aspects are the conjuction, sextile, square, trine, and oppostion.

Athame: Ritual dagger, associated with the air element (pronounced a-the-ma or a-tay´-may).

Birthchart: An astrological chart calculated for the birth of a person, business, town, or other entity; also called a horoscope. It is based on the time, date, and place of birth and shows the positions of the sun, moon, planets, and other astronomical factors.

Book of Shadows: See Grimoire.

Cardinal: A mode by which astrological signs express themselves, usually associated with action; the cardinal signs are Aries, Cancer, Libra, and Capricorn.

Cauldron: Magickal tool connected with feminine creative energy; a kettle or other pot-shaped vessel.

Chakra: Vital energy center, according to Eastern traditions; there are seven major chakras and many smaller ones in the human body.

Chalice: A magickal tool associated with the water element; a ritual cup or goblet.

Charging: A ritual, magickal act to heighten the power of a magick tool or talisman.

Conjunction: Astrological aspect between two or more planets positioned within about seven degrees of each other in a chart.

Cross-Quarter Days: The days when the sun's position is halfway between the equinoxes and the solstices (which are the quarter days). Imbolc, Beltane, Lughnasadh, and Samhain are the cross-quarter days.

Dowsing: A technique for sensing hidden vibrations or objects, often with the aid of a divining tool such as a pendulum or dowsing rod.

Divination: Seeing into the future, often with the help of an oracle or other magickal device.

Druids: Magicians, healers, teachers, high priests, political counselors, and wise ones among the Celts of Ireland, the British Isles, and parts of northern Europe between about 500 B.C.E. and 500 C.E.

Earth: One of the four elements. It is associated with the material realm and physical objects and energies.

Element: A fundamental force in the universe. The four elements are air, earth, fire, and water.

Elementals: Non-physical beings associated with the four elements and the natural world. Air elementals are called sylphs, earth elementals are gnomes, fire elementals are salamanders, and water elementals are undines. Elementals are sometimes confused with fairies.

Ephemeris: A table showing the movements of the heavenly bodies and other astronomical data (pl. ephemerides).

Etheric Body: Subtle energy field that surrounds and permeates the physical body, sometimes called the aura.

Feng Shui: The Chinese art of placement, whereby buildings, rooms, and plots of land are divided into sections called gua, which relate to different areas of life. (Pronounced fung shway.)

Fire: One of the four elements. It is associated with creativity, inspiration, and vitality.

Fixed: A mode by which astrological signs express themselves, usually associated with firmness. The fixed signs are Taurus, Leo, Scorpio, and Aquarius.

Glyph: A symbol or sign.

Golden Dawn: The Hermetic Order of the Golden Dawn, a century-old magickal organization that laid the foundation for modern ceremonial magickal work; based in the mystical traditions of Hebrew Kabbalism, Egyptian magick, and other ancient mystery schools.

Grimoire: A magician's diary of spells, rituals, practices, and results; also called a Book of Shadows.

Horoscope: See birthchart.

House: One of 12 sectors in an astrological chart; each house corresponds to a particular area of life.

I Ching: Ancient Chinese book of wisdom, said to have been composed by Confucius. It is used as an oracle and consists of 64 six-lined symbols, or hexagrams, each of which has a particular meaning. Also called the *Book of Changes*.

Inconjunct: Astrological aspect between two or more planets positioned approximately 147 to 153 degrees apart in a chart; also called a quincunx.

Kabbalah: Ancient system of Hebrew mysticism (alternative spellings include Qabalah, Kabalah, and Cabala).

Knights Templars: An order of knights founded in the 12th century to guard religious pilgrims journeying to Jerusalem. Suppressed officially by the Pope in the 14th century.

Kundalini: A psychic/life force that resides at the base of the spine (root chakra) and that can be aroused through yogic or magickal techniques so that it flows upward to the crown, activating all the chakras. Often likened to a serpent.

Labyrinth: A single, winding pathway of concentric curves or circuits walked for meditative or magickal purposes. A labyrinth's path leads to the center and back out again; unlike a maze, it has no dead ends.

Luminary: The sun or moon (also called lights).

Magician: A person who is aware of the subtle energies that exist all around us and has learned to consciously tap these energies for specific purposes.

Magick: The practice of consciously creating change according to one's will. The "k" is added to distinguish this from stage magic or illusion.

Magick Square: A pattern of squares within squares used in magickal work and linked with the sun, moon, and planets. Each small square contains a number and the squares are configured such that the sum of every row, column, and angle is the same.

Magickal Alphabet: An alphabet whose letters are used in the formation of magickal symbols; generally an alphabet other than the magician's native language. Hebrew, Coptic, Ogham, runes, Enochian, Greek, Egyptian hieroglyphs, and Sanskrit are some of the most popular magickal alphabets.

Mandala: An elaborate, circular image that symbolizes the world and contains archetypal, spiritual, or magickal symbolism. Sanskrit for circle.

Medium Colei: The cusp of the 10th house of an astrological chart, also called midheaven.

Midheaven: The cusp of the 10th house of an astrological chart, also called the medium colei.

Mojo: A magick charm.

Mudra: Ritual movement or gesture.

Mutable: A mode by which astrological signs express themselves, usually associated with flexibility. The mutable signs are Gemini, Virgo, Sagittarius, and Pisces.

Numerology: The study of the symbolic, mystical meanings in numbers.

Occult: Something that is hidden; often associated with ideas, societies, and practices that have been concealed to avoid persecution.

Ogham: Ancient alphabet of the Celts. Each of its 25 letter/symbols is associated with a tree.

Opposition: Astrological aspect between two or more planets positioned approximately 173 to 180 degrees apart in a chart.

Oracle: A device used as a bridge between personal consciousness and higher consciousness, such as the tarot, runes, or the *I Ching*; source of wisdom.

Pagan: One who follows a spiritual path that is closely linked with the natural world and the cosmos, often with a matriarchal or goddess-oriented focus. Witches are an example of Pagans.

Pendulum: A tool used for dowsing; usually a weight suspended from a cord or chain that is sensitive to vibrations and subtle energies.

Pentagram: A five-pointed star associated with protection, the human body, and the earth element.

Planetary Hours: A system of dividing the day and the night into equal parts; each hour is governed by the sun, the moon, or a planet.

Precession of the Equinoxes: At one time, the actual constellations lined up with the astrological signs that bear their names, and the sun (as seen from earth) was at 0 degrees Aries on the Spring Equinox. However, this is no longer true, due to a "wobble" in the earth's motion caused by the gravitational pull of the sun and moon, which each year shifts our position very slightly. The result is that the earth gradually slips backward against the backdrop of the stars and the zodiac belt seems to be advancing or preceding us.

Quarter Days: The solstices and the equinoxes, which divide the solar year into quarters.

Quincunx: See Inconjunct.

Retrogradation: When a planet appears to be moving backward in the sky, as viewed from Earth.

Ritual: A magickal rite or practice that usually includes a prescribed set of movements, words, and/or acts.

Runes: An oracle believed to have originated in northern Europe, also used as an alphabet. The "elder futhark," or early version, of the Norse runes contains 24 symbols or letters; the later Anglo-Saxon futhark has 33. Runes are usually inscribed on pieces of wood, stone, bone, or another hard material. Other languages/scripts, such as Ogham, may also be used as runes.

Sabbat: Holy day or holiday in Pagan traditions. The eight major Sabbats are the solstices, the equinoxes, Imbolc, Beltane, Lughnasadh, and Samhain.

Scrying: The practice of gazing into a glossy surface, usually a black mirror, pool of water, or crystal ball, to see beyond the limits of normal, physical sight.

Seal of Solomon: Six-pointed star formed by the intersection of the alchemical symbols for the elements.

Sephiroth: The spheres or emanations on the Kabbalistic Tree of Life (sing. sephirah).

Sextile: Astrological aspect between two or more planets positioned approximately 54 to 66 degrees apart in a chart.

Shaman: A person who is in touch with the non-physical realms and who can move between the worlds; shamans are able to utilize the energies of the various levels of existence for healing, shapeshifting, and other magickal work.

Shapeshifting: The shamanic practice of changing one's form, usually in spirit or imagination, to that of an animal or other being so as to assume the powers of that being.

Sigil: Magickal symbol composed of letters and/or images to embody a certain concept, abstracted so that it is generally indecipherable by anyone other than its designer.

Smudging: Ritual act of cleansing an area of unwanted energies or vibrations, usually performed with the smoke of burning sage (or other purifying herbs).

Spell: Symbolic act performed while in an altered state of consciousness in order to effect a change.

Square: Astrological aspect between two or more planets positioned approximately 83 to 97 degrees apart in a chart.

Talisman: Magick charm to attract something.

Tarot: An oracle of uncertain origin, usually containing 78 cards that can be used for guidance, meditation, to gain insight into oneself, or to see the future; its archetypes depict all the phases of human existence and evolution.

Transit: The motion of a celestial body through the heavens.

Tree of Life: The Kabbalistic symbol for the fundamental pattern of the universe, it features three triangles, 10 spheres called sephiroth, and 22 paths between them.

Trine: Astrological aspect between two or more planets positioned approximately 113 to 127 degrees apart in a chart.

Void of Course: The period after the moon or a planet makes its last aspect to another heavenly body while it is in a particular zodiacal sign until it enters the next sign; usually an unproductive or inactive period.

Waning moon: The two-week period between the full moon and the new moon, during which the moon is diminishing in size.

Waxing moon: The two-week period between the new moon and the full moon, during which the moon is increasing in size.

Water: One of the four elements. It is associated with the emotions and intuition.

Wheel of the Year: The annual cycle of Sabbats celebrated by Pagans.

Wicca: A Pagan spirituality, sometimes called the Old Religion, which honors the Goddess and the God; followers of this tradition attempt to live in harmony with nature and the cosmos and to do no harm.

Witch: A follower of Wicca; one who attempts to live in accord with the forces of nature and the heavens.

Yang: Archetypal masculine power present in the universe.

Yin: Archetypal feminine power present in the universe.

Zodiac Signs: Twelve divisions of the year based upon the sun's movement through the sky. Aries, Taurus, Gemini, Cancer, Leo, Virgo, Libra, Scorpio, Sagittarius, Capricorn, Aquarius, and Pisces are the 12 signs of the zodiac (literally, circle of animals).

Recommended Reading

Alexander, Skye. *Planets in Signs.* West Chester, Pa.: Whitford Press/Schiffer Publishing, 1988.

Andrews, Ted. *Sacred Sounds.* St. Paul, Minn.: Llewellyn Publications, 1992.

———. *Animal-Speak: The Spiritual and Magical Powers of Creatures Great and Small.* St. Paul, Minn.: Llewellyn Publications, 1996.

Arrien, Angeles. *Signs of Life: The Five Universal Shapes and How to Use Them.* Sonoma, Calif.: Arcus Publishing, 1992.

Arroyo, Stephen. *Astrology, Psychology, and the Four Elements.* Davis, Calif.: CRCS Publications, 1975.

———. *Astrology, Karma, and Transformation.* Davis, Calif.: CRCS Publications, 1978.

Beyerl, Paul, *The Master Book of Herbalism.* Custer, Wash.: Phoenix Publishing, 1984.

Bethards, Betty. *The Dream Book.* Rockport, Mass.: Element Books, 1995.

Bills, Rex E. *The Rulership Book.* Richmond, Va.: Macoy Publishing and Masonic Supply, 1971.

Brady, Bernadette. *The Eagle and the Lark.* York Beach, Maine: Samuel Weiser, 1992.

Buckland, Raymond. *Practical Color Magick.* St. Paul, Minn.: Llewellyn Publications, 1983.

Bunker, Dusty. *Numerology, Astrology, and Dreams.* West Chester, Pa.: Whitford Press/Schiffer Publishing, 1987.

Cunningham, Scott. *Cunningham's Encyclopedia of Magical Herbs.* St. Paul, Minn.: Llewellyn Publications, 1985.

Farber, Monte. *Karma Cards.* New York: Penguin, 1998.

Franklin, Anna, and Paul Mason. *The Sacred Circle Tarot.* St. Paul, Minn.: Llewellyn Publications, 1998.

Greene, Liz. *Saturn.* York Beach, Maine: Samuel Weiser, 1977.

———. *Star Signs for Lovers.* New York: Day Books/Stein and Day, 1980.

———. *The Astrology of Fate.* York Beach, Maine: Samuel Weiser, 1984.

Griffin, Judy. *Mother Nature's Herbal.* St. Paul, Minn.: Llewellyn Publications, 1997.

Hand, Robert. *Planets in Transit.* Rockport, Mass.: Para Research, 1976.

———. *Horoscope Symbols.* Rockport, Mass.: Para Research, 1981.

Hoffman, David. *The New Holistic Herbal.* Boston: Element Books, 1991.

Jung, C. G. *Mandala Symbolism.* Princeton, N.J.: Princeton University Press, 1972.

Knight, Sirona. *Love, Sex, and Magick.* Secaucus, N.J.: Citadel Press, 1999.

Kraig, Donald Michael. *Modern Magick.* St. Paul, Minn.: Llewellyn Publications, 1988.

———. *Modern Sex Magick.* St. Paul, Minn.: Llewellyn Publications, 1999.

Lonegren, Sig. *Labyrinths: Ancient Myths and Modern Uses.* Glastonbury, England: Gothic Image Publications, 1991.

Lüscher, Max. *The Lüscher Color Test.* Trans. by Ian Scott. New York: Pocket Books, 1971.

Mann, A. T. *Life Time Astrology.* Shaftesbury, England: Element Books, 1984.

————. *Astrology and the Art of Healing.* London: Unwin Hyman, 1989.

————. *Sacred Architecture.* Shaftesbury, England: Element Books, 1993.

————. *Sacred Sexuality.* Shaftesbury, England: Element Books, 1995.

Mella, Dorothee L. *Stone Power.* New York: Warner Books, 1986.

Michaud, Debbie. *The Healing Traditions and Spiritual Practices of Wicca.* Los Angeles: Keats Publishing, 2000.

Morwyn. *Secrets of a Witch's Coven.* West Chester, Pa.: Whitford Press/Schiffer Publishing, 1988.

Parker, Derek, and Julia Parker. *The Compleat Astrologer.* New York: McGraw-Hill Book Co., 1971.

Pavitt, William. *The Book of Talismans, Amulets and Zodiacal Gems.* North Hollywood, Calif.: Wilshire Book, 1970.

Regardie, Israel. *The Golden Dawn.* St. Paul, Minn.: Llewellyn Publications, 1986.

Rudhyar, Dane. *The Astrological Houses.* New York: Doubleday, 1972.

Scheffer, Mechthild. *Bach Flower Therapy: Theory and Practice.* Rochester, Vt.: Healing Arts Press, 1988.

Silbury, Lira. *The Sacred Marriage*. St. Paul, Minn.: Llewellyn Publications, 1994.

Simms, Maria. *A Time for Magick*. St. Paul, Minn.: Llewellyn Publications, 2001.

Starhawk. *The Spiral Dance*. San Francisco: Harper and Row, 1979.

Steiner, Rudolf. *How to Know Higher Worlds*. Hudson, N.Y.: Anthroposophical Press, 1994.

Stewart, R. J. *Earth Light*. Rockport, Mass.: Element Books, 1992.

———. *Power within the Land*. Rockport, Mass.: Element Books, 1992.

Sutton, Maya Magee, and Nicholas R. Mann. *Druid Magic*. St. Paul, Minn.: Llewellyn Publications, 2000.

Tisserand, Robert B. *The Art of Aromatherapy*. Rochester, Vt.: Healing Arts Press, 1977.

Tompkins, Peter, and Christopher Bird. *The Secret Life of Plants*. New York: Avon Books, 1972.

Wasserman, James. *Art and Symbols of the Occult*. Rochester, Vt.: Destiny Books, 1993.

Watson, Nancy B. *Practical Solitary Magic*. York Beach, Maine: Samuel Weiser, 1996.

Whitcomb, Bill. *The Magician's Companion*. St. Paul, Minn.: Llewellyn Publications, 1998.

Willis, Tony. *The Runic Workbook*. Northamptonshire, England: Aquarian Press, 1986.

Zerner, Amy, and Monte Farber. *The Enchanted Tarot*. New York: St. Martin's Press, 1990.

Bibliography

Introduction

Parker, Derek, and Julia Parker. *The Compleat Astrologer.* N.Y.: McGraw-Hill, 1971.

Webster's Ninth New Collegiate Dictionary. Springfield, Mass.: Merriam-Webster, 1985.

Whitcomb, Bill. *The Magician's Companion.* St. Paul, Minn.: Llewellyn Publications, 1998.

Chapter 1

Andrews, Ted. *Sacred Sounds.* St. Paul, Minn.: Llewellyn Publications, 1992.

Bills, Rex E. *The Rulership Book.* Richmond, Va.: Macoy Publishing and Masonic Supply Co., 1976.

Gettings, Fred. *The Secret Zodiac.* London: Routledge and Kegan Paul, 1983.

Levan, Michelle. "Medical Astrology." *Dell Horoscope*, vol. 62, no. 9, September 1996.

Mann, A. T. *Sacred Architecture.* Shaftesbury, England: Element Books, 1993.

———. *Astrology and the Art of Healing.* London: Unwin Hyman, 1989.

Parker, Derek, and Julia Parker. *The Compleat Astrologer.* New York: McGraw-Hill, 1971.

Podunovich, Renee. "The Essence of Sales." *New Age Retailer*, vol. 14, no. 2, March/April 2000.

Slevin, Jackie. "Pythagoras: The Father of Numbers." St. Paul, Minn.: *Geocosmic Magazine,* Winter 2000.

Ungar, Anne, and Lillian Huber. *The Horary Reference Book.* San Diego: ACS Publications, 1984.

Whitcomb, Bill. *The Magician's Companion.* St. Paul, Minn.: Llewellyn Publications, 1998.

Chapter 2

Anthony, Carol K. *A Guide to the I Ching.* Stow, Mass.: Anthony Publishing, 1982.

Kraig, Donald Michael. *Modern Magick,* 2nd ed. St. Paul, Minn.: Llewellyn Publications, 1999.

———. *Modern Sex Magick: Secrets of Erotic Spirituality.* St. Paul, Minn.: Llewellyn Publications, 1999.

Mascetti, Manuela Dunn. *Rumi: The Path of Love.* Trans. by Camille and Kabir Helminski. Boston: Element Books, 1999.

Starhawk. *The Spiral Dance.* San Francisco: Harper and Row, 1979.

Steiner, Rudolf. *How to Know Higher Worlds.* Hudson, NY: Anthroposophical Press, 1994.

Tompkins, Peter, and Christopher Bird. *The Secret Life of Plants.* New York: Avon Books, 1973.

Chapter 3

Alexander, Skye. *Planets in Signs.* West Chester, Pa.: Whitford Press/Schiffer Publishing, 1988.

Hand, Robert. *Horoscope Symbols.* Rockport, Mass.: Para Research, 1981.

Rudhyar, Dane. *The Astrological Houses.* New York: Doubleday, 1972.

Chapter 4

Alexander, Skye. *Planets in Signs.* West Chester, Pa.: Whitford Press/Schiffer Publishing, 1988.

Arroyo, Stephen. *Astrology, Psychology, and the Four Elements.* Davis, Calif.: CRCS Publications, 1975.

Greene, Liz. *Star Signs for Lovers.* New York: Day Books/Stein and Day, 1980.

Kelynda. *The Crystal Tree.* West Chester, Pa.: Whitford Press/ Schiffer Publishing, 1987.

Chapter 5

Michaud, Debbie. *The Healing Traditions and Spiritual Practices of Wicca.* Los Angeles: Keats Publishing, 2000.

Starhawk. *The Spiral Dance.* San Francisco: Harper and Row, 1979.

Chapter 6

Starhawk. *The Spiral Dance.* San Francisco: Harper and Row, 1979.

Morwyn. *Secrets of a Witch's Coven.* West Chester, Pa.: Whitford Press/Schiffer Publishing, 1988.

Chapter 7

Beyerl, Paul. *The Master Book of Herbalism.* Custer, Wash.: Phoenix Publishing, 1984.

Mella, Dorothee L. *Stone Power.* New York: Warner Books, 1986.

Pavitt, Kate, and William Thomas. *The Book of Talismans, Amulets and Zodiacal Gems.* North Hollywood, Calif.: Wilshire Book Company, 1970.

Shaw, Ira N. *The Practical Herbalist and Astrologer.* Singapore: Ira N. Shaw, 1970.

Chapter 8

Arrien, Angeles. *Signs of Life: The Five Universal Shapes and How to Use Them.* Sonoma, Calif.: Arcus Publishing, 1992.

Bethards, Betty. *The Dream Book.* Rockport, Mass.: Element Books, 1995.

Bunker, Dusty. *Numerology, Astrology, and Dreams*. West Chester, Pa.: Whitford Press/Schiffer Publishing, 1987.

Lonegren, Sig. *Labyrinths: Ancient Myths and Modern Uses*. Glastonbury, England: Gothic Image Publications, 1991.

Lüscher, Max. *The Lüscher Color Test*. Trans. by Ian Scott. New York: Pocket Books, 1971.

Mann, A. T. *Sacred Architecture*. Shaftesbury, England: Element Books, 1993.

Wasserman, James. *Art and Symbols of the Occult*. Rochester, Vt.: Destiny Books, 1993.

Chapter 9

Barclay, Olivia. *Horary Astrology Rediscovered*. West Chester, Pa.: Whitford Press/Schiffer Publishing, 1990.

Chapter 10

Kraig, Donald Michael. *Modern Magick*. St. Paul, Minn.: Llewellyn Publications, 1988.

Whitcomb, Bill. *The Magician's Companion*. St. Paul, Minn.: Llewellyn Publications, 1998.

Chapter 11

Beyerl, Paul. *The Master Book of Herbalism*. Custer, Wash.: Phoenix Publishing,1984.

Jung, C. G. *Mandala Symbolism*. Princeton, N.J.: Princeton University Press, 1972.

Chapter 12

Hand, Robert. *Planets in Transit*. Rockport, Mass.: Para Research, 1976.

Zerner, Amy and Monte Farber. *The Enchanted Tarot*. New York: St. Martin's Press, 1990.

Index

About the Author

Skye Alexander is also the author of *Planets in Signs* and the award-winning astrological mystery *Hidden Agenda*. She writes for many magazines and almanacs; her stories are included in the anthologies *AstroMysteries* and *Making Love on Cape Ann*. An astrologer, artist, and magickal practitioner for more than two decades, she lives in Gloucester, Massachusetts, with her cats.